THE MAGIC OF YGGDRASILL

D1526547

THE MAGIC OF YGGDRASILL

The Poetry of Old Norse Unconscious

YVES KODRATOFF

Universal Publishers
Irvine • Boca Raton

The Magic of Yggdrasill: The Poetry of Old Norse Unconscious

Universal Publishers, Inc.
Irvine • Boca Raton
USA • 2020
www.Universal-Publishers.com

978-1-62734-290-2 (pbk.)
978-1-62734-291-9 (ebk.)

Typeset by Medlar Publishing Solutions Pvt Ltd, India
Cover design by Ivan Popov

Publisher's Cataloging-in-Publication Data available
at the United States Library of Congress

Names: Kodratoff, Yves, author.
Title: The magic of Yggdrasill : the poetry of Old Norse unconscious / Yves Kodratoff.
Description: Irvine : Universal Publishers, 2020. | Includes bibliographical references.
Identifiers: LCCN 2019057751 (print) | LCCN 2019057752 (ebook) | ISBN 9781627342902 (paperback) | ISBN 9781627342919 (ebook)
Subjects: LCSH: Old Norse poetry--History and criticism. | Eddas--History and criticism. | Magic in literature.
Classification: LCC PT7170 .K63 2020 (print) | LCC PT7170 (ebook) | DDC 839/.61009--dc23
LC record available at https://lccn.loc.gov/2019057751
LC ebook record available at https://lccn.loc.gov/2019057752

Contents

Chapter III How Much Reliable is the Poetic Edda? **119**

Chapter IV   Four Archetypal Images Carried by Hávamál and Völuspá

Foreword

This book started with the author's realization that what Old Norse calls 'magic' can be understood as 'unconscious', stated as being a mild obviousness by C. G. Jung. Here is Jung's (2014—first ed. 1960) citation p. 374, § 725: the ancients ones instituted "highly important rites between childhood and adulthood … for the quite unmistakable purpose of effecting the separation from the parents by magical means. This institution would be entirely superfluous if the relation to parents were not felt to be equally magical…" Immediately after follows the statement:

"But "magical" means everything where unconscious influences are at work."

Since Old Norse poetry, we have used here, evokes 'magic' instead of 'unconsciousness', we will keep this way of speech throughout the book. Chapter 4 will provide examples where 'unconscious Norse archetypes' are analyzed with a more modern vocabulary, including Jung himself when he analyses goddess Frigg's behavior.

This study will lead us to unveil another aspect of our half unconscious-half conscious psyche, the one of the plural '*sköp*' sent by magicians. These modern *sköp* amount to a so claimed conscious advertisement and propaganda under their multiple forms.

The Magic of Yggdrasill in the Poetic Edda: *A Poetry of Old Norse Unconscious*

The present book aims at three logically connected targets:

- spotting stanzas using a vocabulary clearly calling upon magic for improving our knowledge of ancient Norse magic,
- checking that no convincing proof of 'Christian influences' on Poetic Edda had been provided by the academic community,
- spotting a few images of Old Norse unconscious archetypes

leading to unexpected finds

of natural instances of the Eddaic meter Galdralag (§ IV-1 and 2) and the concluding 'good luck' Galdralag

Our first aim is highlighting some aspects of Norse magic that exist in the Poetic Edda, though most translations are not really able to reveal them because they must use a modern vocabulary in which the religious aspects of life took the better over the magic ones, the last being most often ridiculed. In particular, in chapter II, we shall see how the role of tree Yggdrasill in Norse Magic is strongly evoked in most translations of a famous Eddaic Poem, Völuspá, relating its progressive destruction while Ragnarök takes place. This explains the title, "the Magic of Yggdrasill," of this book.

The first two chapters of the book are dedicated to this goal. Chapter I describes several types of Norse magic and it explains the links among different magic behaviors. Chapter II provides the basic necessary documentation, that is, the Eddaic poetic stanzas the vocabulary of which alludes to magic. We give their Old Norse (ON) version, a possible translation into English and the explications necessary to bring out their magic content. In many cases, each word loaded with a magic content can be understood by its context in the stanza. In some cases, the context of the stanza needs to be replaced into the larger context of the whole poem or even in the global one of Eddaic Poetry. This literary study will enable us to detail (in § II conclusions) the meaning of the *sköp* used in this poetry, up to the point to observe their modern counterpart that we will call 'advertisement-propaganda' in our conclusion on sköp.

That we rely so heavily on Eddaic poetry leads us to question its reliability as being a proper image of the various pre-Christian civilizations that cohabited in pagan Scandinavia. This will be debated in Chapter III. This third chapter, while it refutes the huge amount of literature dedicated to spotting non-Norse influences, mainly Christian ones, on Eddaic poetry, tries also to give a few insights of the vitally important role of magic in the Old Norse world. Some of our arguments may however look somewhat low level when it happens that the arguments to refute were very superficial ones which, unfortunately, seems to make them all the more convincing. As opposed to the presently widespread opinion, this chapter will show that poetic Edda stands quite firm in front of the suspicions of 'Christian influences' as soon as the suspicious minds have to prove their claims instead of juggling with 'obvious', 'obviously' and the behavior of supposedly 'devout 13rd century Christians'.

It is quite clear that the bulk of this poetry relies on pagan beliefs and behaviors. To cite only one such flabbergasting 'pagan' detail, we will see in chapter II-9 (about Fáfnismál) that Sigurðr drinks the blood of both Reginn and Fáfnir after he killed them: *drakk blóð þeira beggja, Regins ok Fáfnis* (word for word: 'drank blood their both, of Reginn and of Fáfnir').

Two poems, namely Hávamál and Völuspá, have been put under heavy suspicions of Christian influences. We shall explain why this assertion is ludicrous for Hávamál and far from as obvious as it is usually claimed for Völuspá.

Our third target is to use this 'confirmed first hand pagan information' in order to deepen our knowledge of Old Norse civilization. Chapter IV is an illustration of the type of information on this civilization that can be

General Introduction

This book attempts to analyze the concepts of örlög and sköp (both plural) as we find them implicitly defined in ON texts that use them. At once, a doubt could be thrown on using these texts. This doubt can be stated as did a US forum called 'Heathen Discussion' on Dec. 6th 2018. "The question is: Being transcribed hundreds of years later during Christian times by devout Christians is it transcribed truly and unchanged?" The very way the question is stated by heathen people themselves implies a 'reasonable' negative answer. This topic will be treated in depth in the third chapter of this book in order to justify a more complex and positive answer. Until then, let us try to observe what örlög and sköp may mean.

This analysis asks for a quite large amount of information. We could not yet complete it on the saga corpus, which thus remains a task to come. It used the whole Eddaic corpus, and for the sagas, 96 sagas including all the traditional ones. The number of available documents is large enough to lead to some clear conclusions. The translations are mine, but they have been compared with existing translations that tend to forget the importance of magic in Old Norse worldview.

The quotations of the words örlög and sköp are always given in context, with a few lines of the poem that make it possible to understand their meaning or meanings.

For these translations, we used de Vries' etymological dictionary (published in German only—in short: 'deVries'), Cleasby-Vigfusson' Icelandic-English dictionary (CV) and also very often, Lexicon Poëticum antiquæ linguæ septentrionalis of Sveinbjörn Egilsson (We used the original version in Latin language and not Finnur Jonsson's Danish edition—in short LexPoet). This last provides the meaning of a greater number of words than CV, associated to a wealth of quotations illustrating the use of the words, mainly in poetry.

Here is the order of the poems some stanzas of which will be used in the following:

Völuspá, Hávamál, Vafþrúðnismál, Grímnismál, Lokasenna, Alvíssmál, Helgakviða hundingsbana hin fyrri, Völundarkviða, Grípisspá, Fáfnismál, Sigrdrífumál, Reginsmál, Sigurðarkviða in skamma, Guðrúnarkviða in fyrsta, Guðrúnarkviða in forna, Oddrúnarkviða (Oddrúnargrátr), Atlakviða (Dauði Atla), Atlamál in grænlenzku, Grógaldr, Fjölsvinnsmál, Hrafnagaldur Óðins.

An unexpected consequence of this magic orientated skimming through poetic Edda is bringing forth an original view of it, one less warlike than the usual ones, though terribly impressive as Chapter II will hopefully illustrate.

We will analyze the meaning of a little more than 60 stanzas belonging to the poetic Edda. This leads to a dispersion of attention that tends to concentrate on the current stanza, and somewhat forgets the other ones. In order to avoid this dispersion, the following introduction plays the role of a kind of guide to our journey among these stanzas by providing us some advance information that will be rediscovered and detailed during this journey. We will need to reach our conclusion of chapters I and II in order to completely justify this guide. It will then become a detailed and argued chart of the main actors of magic in Poetic Edda and a valuable approximation of the magical sides of ON civilization.

Poetic Edda is our principal source of knowledge on **örlög**[1] but it also quite often uses two other words: **sköp**, also met in the sagas, and **rök**. Less often, fate is named **mjötuðr** or **urðr**. This last word is also Norn Urðr's name: we will meet several examples of this use.

On *örlög*

The traditional spelling of this word is **ørlǫg**. The one provided by CV, **örlög** (it will be used in this book) simplifies, with no confusion, the correct spelling. Note nevertheless that the first editors (before Finnur Jónsson) had

---

[1] (ørlög, plural of *ørlag*—*lag* is a layer), i.e. a structure defining a vertical order when stacking up several layers.

no fixed rule. For example, Rask (1818) spells it as '***avrlavg***', and Möbius (1860) and Egilsson (1860) as '***orlög***'.

The neutral substantive *ørlag* (spelled here as *örlag*) means 'closing, ending' and its plural, *ørlǫg (örlög)* means 'destiny, death, combat'.

On *sköp*

The neutral substantive *skap* indicates the state or the mood of a person. But it is also associated to verb *skapa* meaning 'to shape'. This is why its plural, *sköp* took the meaning of 'shapings', i.e. of everything that shapes our life, our fate. In the following, we will keep the Norse word *örlög* which is well-known or it will be translated, if necessary, by 'destiny' or 'fate'. The word *sköp*, conversely, is quasi unknown and it will be systematically translated by "shapings" in order to avoid confusing it with destiny, with the modern meaning of this word.

Our life takes its course along such shapings. They are carried out, with more or less softness, by our parents, our friends, our passions. When our mother softly explains that "you should not behave in this way…" she gently shapes us. When a wizard casts a spell, when someone is tortured, both wizard and torturer carry out brutish shapings. When an advertisement catches your eye, it exerts so-called 'sub-liminal' shapings on your future customer behavior.

In the following, we will slowly access these principles of Heathen spirituality and will look further into the difference between örlög and *sköp*.

It is also necessary to add a few words about ***sköpuð***, past participle of verb *skapa*, and on its preterit ***skóp*** (he/she shaped). We will meet below nine occurrences of *sköpuð* and 4 of *skóp* which always take place in a context either of explicit magic of destiny shapings, or in the majestic context of the world creation. The only occurrence which can be seen as a material shaping is found in Völuspá stanza 7 saying that the gods "*tangir skópu* (they shaped tongs)," though the materiality of such tongs could be disputed…

On *rök*

This word became famous because of *ragna-rök*, the gods' *rök* that Snorri Sturluson (and more recently, Wagner) understood as being the word *rökkr* or *rökr*: darkness, twilight. Other sources (among which Poetic Edda) led the experts to understand it as *rök* (it is then a plural without singular) meaning: causes, signs, explanations, the course of things, fate. The multiplicity of these meanings does not enable to learn a clear lesson on the nature of *rök* in the ancient Germanic world. We will clear up this problem after having studied 4 characteristic examples of them.

We will meet two more words possibly translated as 'fate':

Mjötuðr, is the 'measure-supplier' or 'master of the good measure'. We meet this word five times in poetic Edda. We will not be able to fully explain the use of this word before commenting on Sigurðarkviða in skamma § II-12. Since the Norse poetic language tends to avoid repeating the same word, a necessary repetition is often done by using a metaphorical form called *heiti*, a metaphor related to a single word, or a *kenning*: a metaphor using several words. This is particularly striking for *mjötuðr*: we will insist on the difference between an occurrence of 'word' *mjötuðr* and an occurrence of a heiti or a kenning for it. We shall call the last an occurrence of the 'idea' of *mjötuðr* that tells the reader that the concept of *mjötuðr* is provided through a heiti or a kenning.

Auðna, 'luck', met in stanza 98 of Atlamál in grænlenzku. This word evokes 'chance' with the modern meaning of 'fortunate coincidence'.

Note on the references: in the following, when we refer to translations of Hávamál, Völuspá or Hrafnagaldur Óðins, unless explicitly stated, we point at our web-available translations indicated in the references section by 'Hávamál' or 'Völuspá or 'Hrafnagaldur Óðins'.

CHAPTER I

Magic and Divine Beings and Heroes

This chapter deals with eight characters around which magic is gathered in the Poetic Edda:

I-1. Norns as mistresses of *örlög*

I-2. Yggdrasill [**name of the Northern world tree**] as a *mjötuðr* ('measurer')

I-3. Yggdrasill and the end of Æsir's magic [**the plural word 'æsir' is the name of a family of Northern gods such as Óðinn ('Odin'), Þórr ('Thor or Tor'), Freyja etc.**]

    I-3.1. The six (or seven?) occurrences of the idea of *mjötuðr* in Völuspá.

    I-3.2. Consequence of the six first occurrences of the idea of *mjötuðr* in Völuspá.

I-4. Óðinn and his handling of the gender problem

I-5. Yggdrasill seen as a provider of Óðinn's magic

I-6. Humankind's two weaknesses: *Örlöglauss ok lítt megandi*

I-7. A female heroic character: Brynhildr (formerly known as Sigrdrífa)

I-8. A male heroic character: Sigurðr as his father's avenger

I-1. Norns as *örlög* rulers

At first, here are a few words on the relationship between Roman Parcae and Norse Norns.

Greek mythology calls Moirai the three goddesses who spin our destiny. The word *moira* means someone in charge of assigning the result of a draw, an 'allotter' and also 'fate'. This recalls Norse *mjötuðr* who "allots the measure," often translated as "measurer of destiny."

The Moirai are Clotho (Spinner), Lachesis (Allotter) and Atropos (Unescapable one). The three corresponding Latin goddesses, Parcae (Fates), are called Nona (she spins our lives, 'Spinner'), Decima (she measures the thread of our lives and credits us with a lifetime, 'Measurer') and Morta (she inexorably cuts the thread of our lives, 'Unescapable'). The functions of the Parcae thus correspond directly to the Moirai's from which they derive.

The role of the three Norns is (almost) universally compared to the Moirai's and Parcae's, for example in Wikipedia English version: "they roughly correspond to other controllers of humans' destiny." A disputed convention connects them to the triplet 'past, present, future' because of an academic traditional interpretation of their names.

First, notice that *mjötuðr* could indeed match Greek Lachesis and Latin Decima. It seems, however, that *mjötuðr* is a power aside from the Norns and the names of the three Norns are well-known and do not directly imply the notion of measure.

In the second part of this book, in § II-1.4, we will analyze the name of the Norns by commenting on Völuspá stanza 20. We will reach the following conclusions:

- Urðr's name analysis suggests a person who, as a doctor or a financial controller provides a balance sheet. She is responsible for judging how gods, humankind, or individuals were, are and will be able to manage their existence.
- Verðandi is the "active authority" who decides how all actors of our universe have acted, act and will act in the light of Urðr's assessments.
- Skuld's name tells us that, with the help of Verðandi, she takes care that each of the past 'debts' will be repaid in the future.

The Latin influence nevertheless appeared as 'obvious' to a lot of people, and this explains the mass of drawings representing the Norns as spinners. This popular error should not too much impress us. Basically, the Romans, followed by the Christians, imagined their Fates as spinners and we are naturally under the influence of these two civilizations, much more than ON civilization has been before Christianization.

It seems that, all things considered, the main problem is that, when we think of destiny, we tend to actually think of our personal destiny, which is terribly insignificant: coarsely speaking, we are going to die one day, we know that we cannot do anything against it, and that's it.

Let us rather think of humankind's destiny, some features of which were revealed during the 20th century, such as global warming and decline in biodiversity. We are more and more convinced that global warming (among others) is happening right now: in a sense it seems to be humankind's fate to undergo such a global warming. What can we do about it? Well, there are a thousand global reactions to oppose a catastrophic warming and a thousand other individual ones to live this warming, catastrophic or not, so as to suffer as little as possible.

Ancient Norse people believed that when the Norns had made a decision, nothing could oppose to it. Norns, however, did not decide of each small detail, they did leave some freedom to humankind to decide several aspects of its fate.

We may thus imagine that **ON** civilization, being unaware of the warming causes, would thus react in attempting to fill up the possible holes in örlög by shaping magic incantations called *sköp* ('shapings'), available to their gods and to humankind. This behavior might obviously fail to be approved nowadays, though effectively 'cursing off human ones' who are causing global warming may be an efficient way to oppose to them.

On its part, our civilization, as completely aware of all the causes as it is, up to now tried to fight against this warming by organizing assemblies that are clearly more incantatory than decisive.

Which standpoint of the two is the best one? We should at first note that our political leaders' incantations address our conscious psyche while örlög and *sköp* obviously address our unconscious one. It is also obvious that global warming is caused by our (conscious) behaviors driven by our unconscious urges. Thus, 'communicating' with our unconscious psyche, as psychiatry does, might be vastly more efficient than addressing the conscious one. In other words, we suggest that global warming is due to one of humankind's psychoses, namely the unconscious urge that tells us: "if you do not fit well with your environment, do change it!" Since this way of thinking is one of the typical parts of the acknowledged psychosis features, are we going to do better that what Norse *sköp* would do?

I-2. Yggdrasill as *Mjötuðr* ('Measurer')

The fact that Yggdrasill is a form of deity for the ancient Norse is quite 'obvious'. But on which texts to rely? What are its attributes and what is its place in the Nordic pantheon? We will try to answer at least partially these questions.

We will find, at the end of this section, the meanings provided for *mjötuðr* by the dictionaries and those adopted by some translators.

The word *mjötuðr* shows a multitude of meanings that revolve around 'who makes the decisions', especially with respect to people life and death. This explains the meaning adopted in modern translations: "fate," a word that has lost enough of its magic in our civilization to be accepted by everyone. Just as *sköp, sköpuð* and their derivatives, we can safely assume that the ancient Norse did not forget the magic associated to all these words. We must therefore reintroduce ancient times magic to understand 'from within' their exact meaning as they are used in the Poetic Edda.

We all know that Scandinavian mythology deals with four 'races', or rather families of deities: gods, giants, elves and dwarves. We must nevertheless add Norns who, although probably of giant's descent, manipulate a special magic imposing all its decrees, those of örlög. There is also a considerable crowd of somewhat immaterial beings named 'spirits' in whom our civilization no longer believes. These vaguely correspond to the *vættir* (one *vættr*, two *vættir*) and the *landvættir*. To complete this picture, it must be remembered that the dead ones' souls are often included among the *vættir*. The purpose of this section is to describe an additional divine 'family' that contains a single individual, Yggdrasill whose status is comparable to the Norns'.

We meet five occurrences of word *mjötuðr* in the poetic Edda, two in Völuspá, one in Sigurðarkviða in skamma stanza (s.) 71, Oddrúnarkviða s. 14 and Fjölsvinnsmál s. 18. In § I-3, 'Ragnarök and Yggdrasill', we will, following Völuspá way of speech, argue that *mjötuðr* is one of the 6 words by which the völva designates Yggdrasill. This shows us that *mjötuðr* is at least one facet of Yggdrasill's roles.

One saga only, among the 95 that were collected, contains the word *mjötuðr, Hervarar ok Heiðreks saga*[2] (available at 'Hervör's myth'). Just before

---

[2] Carolyne Larrington included this poem in her presentation of the Poetic Edda (2014 version, pp. 268–273).

she leaves her ('dead') father Angantýr after getting from him his magic sword, he tells her:

Þú skalt eiga	You will own
ok una lengi,	and long time enjoy it,
hafðu á huldu	if you keep it secret (carefully)
Hjálmars bana;	Hjálmar's death (the sword that killed Hjálmar)
takattu á eggjum,	do not touch it by its edges,
eitr er í báðum,	both are poisoned,
sá er manns	it is of someone's **mjötuðr** (death, fate or
mjötuðr	measurer) *Larrington: "a man's fate-measurer"*
meini verri.	by malignant wound.
Far vel, dóttir,	Farewell, daughter (more or less implying 'dear daughter')
fljótt gæfak þér	quite quickly I gave you
tólf manna fjör,	of twelve men's vitality,
ef þú trúa mættir,	if faith you meet (you keep, you live with);
afl ok eljun,	strength and energy,
allt it góða,	all that (was) good,
þat er synir Arngríms	(that) Arngrím's son (Arngrím is Angantýr's father)
at sik leifðu.	left as inheritance.

You see that here, too, the choice to translate *mjötuðr* by death or fate partially destroys the poetic value of these verses that attribute a magical role to this poison that remains, forever, mysteriously stuck to the blade of a magic sword. Larrington has probably been aware of it and did translate *mjötuðr* by 'fate-measurer' instead of a flat 'death'.

To conclude, let us say that even when facing the kind of destructive madness that seems to be taking hold of our current civilization, we may notice that the need to avoid eliminating trees (i.e. the need to reforest) seems to be one of the very first 'measure' on which humankind has agreed, quite before the still non-existent limitations to global warming: An unconscious '*mjötuðr*' effect?

Meanings of mjötuðr *in some dictionaries*

CV (common usage): meaning 1: 'master of the measure'—meaning 2: 'doom'.

deVries (meaning related to etymology): '*Schicksalsbeherrscher* (master of destiny), *Schicksal* (fate), *Tod* (death)'.

LexPoet (use in poetry): '*sector* (chopper), *gladius* (sword), *mors* (death), *arbor Yggdrasill* (Yggdrasill tree), *omnium rerum principio* (everything principle)'.

Classical translations of mjötuðr

(if unspecified, these translations are in the context of Sigurðarkviða in skamma s. 71 as described by § II-12)

Simrock (Die Edda) 1851: '*der Gott*' (God); http://www.thomasnesges.de/edda/.

Thorpe (Elder Edda) 1866: 'sword' (the sword with which Brynhildr commits suicide).

Finnur Jónsson, (De Gamle Eddadigte), 1932, p. 182 (footnote): 'døden' (death).

Belows (Poetic Edda, 1936) Internet, Sacred Texts: ('fate').

Auden & Taylor (Norse poems, 1969): 'ruler of fate'.

Boyer (Poetic Edda, 1992): '*destin*'.

Orchard (Elder Edda, 2011): 'fate'.

Larrington (The Poetic Edda) 1994, revised 2014
  - Völuspá s. 2 (*miötviðr*): Measuring-Tree.
  - Völuspá s. 45 (*miötuðr*): Measuring-Tree.
  - Sigurðarkviða in skamma: 'fate'.
  - Oddrúnarkviða: 'fate'.
  - Fjölsvinnsmál s. 22 (her numbering): 'Measuring-Tree'.
  - Waking of Angantýr p. 272, s. 29: 'fate-measurer'.

I-3. Yggdrasill and the end of Æsir's magic

When we, users of internet groups devoted to Old Norse religions, talk about Ragnarök, the majority is willing to admit that some gods are killed during this disaster, but the same are often reluctant to admit Yggdrasill's disappearance. It has been only when becoming aware of the magic content of Völuspá [**Seeress' foreseeing – ON word for seeress is völva and 'of a seeress' is rendered by "völu"**] that it became obvious how much we were mistaken. When analyzing the meaning of völva's words and imparting to them a mystical value (and therefore a magic one in the ancient Norse civilization), it becomes possible to argue that the völva speaks six times of Yggdrasill, in stanzas 2 (*miötvið mœran*: measure-tree famous), 19 (*Yggdrasill*), 27 (*undir helgom baðmi*: under the sacred tree), 46 (*miötuðr*: measure-ruler), 47 (*ascr Yggdrasils*: ash-tree (of) Yggdrasill), 57 (*við aldrnara*: along ancient nourisher). This succession describes how Yggdrasill is progressively destroyed by Surtr's fire.

As a side remark, let us note a possible though less certain seventh instance in s. 60, thus in the gods' residence after Ragnarök, Gimlé, as explained at the end of § I-3.2.

I-3.1. The six first occurrences of the idea of mjötuðr in Völuspá

As already noticed, an Eddaic poem should not repeat the word Yggdrasill 6 times: the repetitions are done by using metaphorical forms called *heiti*, metaphors of a single word, or *kenningar* (several words). If a translator neglects this mystical allusion and translates it by a mundane word, then the deep meaning of the stanza escapes the reader and any allusion to magic is hidden.

The most typical example is that of stanza 2 (s. 2) where the völva uses the word *miötvið* which means *miöt-viðr* = measure-tree, tree of the measure. Cleasby-Vigfusson declares that this form is undoubtedly due to a copyist error. Since this word appears with two slightly different but similar spellings in two famous manuscripts, Codex Regius and Hauksbók, that largely differ on some other verses, a copyist error seems to be out of the question. The existence of this word in the Norse language thus cannot be denied. Yggdrasill can be a "tree of measure" even if this way of speech appears twice only in skaldic poetry.

Let us then follow the variations of the vocabulary designating Yggdrasill during Ragnarök, as told by Völuspá.

s. 2, the völva evokes ancient times. She says (literally):

nío man ec heima,	nine remember I countries
nío ivíði	nine Giantesses (or ogresses)
miötvið mœran	the <u>measure-tree</u> famous
fyr mold neðan	toward the ground under.

Mjötviðr is therefore a standard kenning for Yggdrasill as long as Ragnarök has not yet begun. It represents all the natural forces that are favorable to humans and their gods, while the Giants represent dangerous and unfavorable forces to humankind and gods.

In s. 19, Ragnarök is not yet started and this stanza highlights one of Yggdrasill's functions. There still exists an idyllic environment on earth.

Ask veit ek standa,	An ask-tree know-I stands,
heitir Yggdrasill,	called Yggdrasill,
hár baðmr, ausinn	high tree, sprinkled
hvíta auri;	with white mud;
þaðan koma döggvar	wherefrom come the dews
þærs í dala falla,	that fall in the vale,
stendur æ yfir grænn	it stands up always green
Urðar brunni.	above Urðr's source.

s. 27: Here is the first allusion to Ragnarök, but it is done as if 'nothing happened yet'. It only points out that Heimdall's horn, with which he will call the gods to Ragnarök battle, is still in its place. Yggdrasill is called here the "sacred tree."

Veit hón Heimdalar	She knows (that) Heimdall's
hlióð um fólgit	noisy horn has been entrusted
undir heiðvönom	to the 'in lack of serenity'
helgom baðmi;	sacred tree;

Until then, Yggdrasill remains the sacred tree. Note nevertheless the two implied threats, the one carried by Gjallarhorn and Yggdrasill's "need of serenity." It is precisely about to lose its serenity since 19 stanzas later we will learn that it starts burning.

s. 46 marks the beginning of Ragnarök:

Leica Míms synir,	Mímir's sons move about
enn miötuðr kyndiz	and the <u>measure-ruler</u> burns
at ino gamli	within it old
Giallarhorni;	Gjallahorn;
hátt blæss Heimdallr.	the beat blows Heimdall (Heimdallr blows the beat)

The last three lines mean that "Heimdall blows the beat (of Ragnarök) with ancient Gjallarhorn": Heimdall is in tune with the measure ruler, Yggdrasill.

Here is another example of interpreted translations hiding the presence of Yggdrasill: Boyer and Orchard, for instance, translates *miötuðr* by "destiny" and thus hide an occurrence of Yggdrasill-Mjötuðr.

s. 47 indicates Yggdrasill's first sufferings:

Scelfr Yggdrasils	Shakes Yggdrasill
ascr standandi,	the standing ash-tree
ymr iþ aldna tré,	moans the old tree
enn iötunn losnar;	and the giant (Fenrir) gets loose; [**Fenrir is the name of a huge wolf who has been magically chained by the Æsir**]

s. 57: Yggdrasill is entirely on fire. It is no longer a sacred tree nor a measure-master but a dying old tree.

geisar eimi	rage the fumes
við aldrnara,	along ancient-fosterer (or former feeder, i.e. Yggdrasill)
leicr hár hiti	plays high the heat,
við himin siálfan	until the sky itself.

Yggdrasill is now nothing more than a gigantic torch and the flames running along its trunk rise to the sky. Again, to eliminate this 'cumbersome' Yggdrasill, the community of translators found nothing better than to see "fire" in this 'former feeder' under the pretext that fire is used to cook the food … which is true but totally out of Ragnarök context.

The example of Dronke's translation (her s. 54) is typical: "Fumes rage against fire,/fosterer of life, …" which does of 'fire' a 'fosterer of life', which is an angelic and ridiculous vision that sees the immense fire that is destroying our universe as a comfy home fire.

I-3.2. *Yggdrasill*, mjötuðr *and ON magic*

In this section, our aim will be to show that the whole body of ON magic revolves around Yggdrasill, which at last will enable us to justify the title of this book putting Yggdrasill in the position of being pivotal to Norse magic. This rather unclassical claim finds it roots in I-3.1 We provide there an original view on the meaning of Völuspá by tracking the occurrences of a heiti for 'Yggdrasill', namely *mjötuðr*, that we claim to appear six times in the poem.

At first, let us have a look upon Völuspá structure from the point of view of Yggdrasill. Its first verse is a ritual formula used to ask silence at the beginning of the Icelandic general meeting, or before declaiming poetry: It conveys no information specific to the mythological content of the whole poem. Stanza 2 actually begins what we can call 'Ragnarök's saga'. Its last two lines speak of

Miötvið mæran	the measure-master (= Yggdrasill) famous
fyr mold neðan.	toward the ground under.

The real tale therefore starts with a stanza citing a 'baby' Yggdrasill, in the first stages of its growth.

Now, near the end of the poem and accepting that the 'ancient fosterer' of stanza 57 is a burning Yggdrasill as suggested in § I-3.1, we recognize here an Yggdrasill in the last stage of its existence. The following stanza 58 is a mere repetition of s. 44, that is to say a slightly vacuous stanza, that ends Ragnarök's saga since the following stanzas 58 to 66 tell us of the new world to come after Ragnarök. It follows that the proper story of Ragnarök shows a nice symmetrical structure:

[non-significant stanza followed by Yggdrasill's speaking stanza] ←→
  [Yggdrasill's speaking stanza followed by non-significant stanza]

Nobody can thus dispute that this structure puts Yggdrasill in an outstanding position within the poem. We could even express this as an indication that Æsir's magic starts exactly when Yggdrasill grows up, and ends exactly when Yggdrasill disappears.

We will analyze the message carried by the last eight stanzas in chapter III since the world they describe has been systematically understood as the coming of Christianity, and the magic they possibly carry is no longer the one of the Æsir.

A third argument is relative to the kind of equivalence that Völuspá implies between the word *yggdrasill* and the word *mjötuðr*.

That the Norse word *mjötuðr* carries a magic halo is made obvious by its Anglo-Saxon use: We note that, in the 'Christian Norse language', its positive meaning of 'measurer' is used, though much less often than its negative meaning of plague. Anglo-Saxon conversion to Christianity took place some four centuries before the one of Norse people, thus Christianity much less influenced Norse language than the Anglo-Saxon one. The last contains a word equivalent to Norse *mjötuðr*, namely *meotud* or *metod* meaning 'fate, God, Christ', showing that the Anglo-Saxon word keeps the positive aspect only of this 'measurer'. Its negative, devilish aspect, is expressed by the word *metodsceaft*: (creation/construction of *metod*) meaning: 'fate edict, disaster, death'. The only Norse equivalent to *metodsceaft* is *mjötuðr* when it carries the meaning of plague. This move from Heathen magic to a Christian mystical fervor shows that the Heathen Anglo-Saxons have been conscious of the positive magic of *metod* and of the negative one of *metodsceaft*.

It is thus quite clear that the Anglo-Saxon Christians refused to mix up in the same word a godly and a devilish being. On the contrary, since the Norse Christians did not seem to have felt something heretic in their double faced *mjötuðr*, we may guess that the two faces of the measure-master have been suggested by some incredibly ancient, half-forgotten belief the incongruity of which had been lost in the mists of the past. An obvious companion to this double-sided character is giant born Loki who has been actively destructive while Yggdrasill 'negative side' did not go further than generating some fear by being *ýgr* (fierce), or the *drasill* (horse) of *yggr-* or *uggr-* (both mean 'anxious'), i.e. a carrier of anxiety. In addition, and less strongly touched by this ability to generate fear, we find Óðinn himself, also called fearful and fear carrier in one of his many facets.

Völuspá makes it obvious that the Æsir should have been warier of ambiguous, often clowning Loki who ultimately belongs to the world of the Giants since he participates in Ragnarök on their side. Inversely, Yggdrasill and Óðinn are both destroyed during Ragnarök together with humankind: All belong to the same divine world built by the Æsir. This may explain why the fearful side of *mjötuðr* has been kept as a *heiti* for Yggdrasill whose fearfulness is however not underlined in the Poetic Edda.

We should also notice that Yggdrasill is never described as an acting magician: it cannot send *sköp* as humans and gods do or allot a destiny as Norns do. Being a measure provider, it seems to be able to fix limits to the magic power of gods and people. This can be linked to the fact that Óðinn, who learned rune magic within Yggdrasill's aura, feels necessary to insist on the limits of magic in Hávamál s. 145 where he states:

ON text	Literal translation in pseudo-English
Betra er óbeðit	Better he does not ask for
in sé ofblótit,	than over-sacrificing to the gods,
ey sér til gildis gjöf;	ever (might) you be (*or* to you) to the proper value the gift
betra er ósent	Better he does not dispatch (and even kills)
en sé ofsóit.	than to 'over-used' (magic, possibly up to 'wiping out').

Note on the meaning of *ofsóit*: it reads as *of—sóit* where 'of' is an intensifier ('very much so') to the verb that follows and *sóit* is the preterit of *sóa*, to make use of something, here "he had too much made use, or wiped out the victims of magic."

The first two lines address humankind: they advise to avoid begging the gods and over-sacrificing to them. The last two lines may concern both gods and humankind: better avoiding to send curses to your enemies than wiping them out by means of magic. These four lines thus advise respect to a measure, as a master measurer as Yggdrasill might do.

Note on a possible seventh occurrence of 'mjötuðr' in s. 60 (*þinurr or þinull?*)

Stanza 60 belongs to this part of Völuspá which provides a few hints on the way the "new world" of Gimlé will be:

60.	Literal translation
Finnaz æsir	Have just met the æsir
á Iðavöllr	on Iðavöllr [Fulfillments Plain]
*og um **moldþinur***	and about ground-pine_tree *OR* ground-rope [Yggdrasill OR Jörmun-gandr = 'Gigantic-staff' that encircles Earth]
mátcan, dœma	powerful, judge/chat
oc minnaz þar	and recall
á megindóma	of the great judgments
oc á Fimbultýs	and on Fimbultýr's
fornar rúnar.	ancient runes.

In traditional translations (as Dronke's, Larrington's and Orchard's), the translators read '*þinull*' instead of *þinurr* as given in the manuscript. '*Þinull*' is a rope bordering a net, and this 'rope' suggests to see a kenning for Jörmungandr in *moldþinurr*. If we keep the manuscript spelling, we read *þinurr*, a pine-tree, and this 'tree' suggests a kenning for Yggdrasill.

We may suppose that, Yggdrasill being burned off, the commentators believed that it 'should' no longer exist in Gimlé. It hence was much more 'logical' to see here a kenning for Jörmungandr than one for Yggdrasill. Now, if we remember that at the beginning of the times, in s. 2, the "famous measure-tree" is still *mold neðan* (under the earth), we are untitled to read here a hint for a link between s. 2 and s. 60, that is: at the beginning of the post-ragnarök times, the existence of a *moldþinurr* (instead of the *moldþinull* introduced by the commentators) is mostly expected. The word used in the manuscripts, *þinurr*, should then have been be carefully kept as such since it announces the presence of a growing 'baby Yggdrasill' intended to allot the measure in Gimlé when it will be full-grown.

This interpretation strongly suggests that the new world was 'behaving' in a way similar to the old world one. It follows that, instead being similar to an apocalypse to be compared to the Christian one, Völuspá could rather describe a kind of reincarnation of the old Earth into a new one, Gimlé. Which influences may have been at work here is not relevant to the present work, except that it excludes a Christian one.

I-4. Óðinn and his handling of the gender problem

This section is far from dealing with all the various aspects of Óðinn's magic. Its aim is to put his magic in a light different from the one usually attributed to him. In other words, we are quite aware that Óðinn's magic carries an 'aura' of wickedness which at least partly relies on his supposed scorn for femininity. Once this kind of suspicion will be removed, we will be able to understand Hávamál many warnings relative to feminine magic as they actually are: marks of respect for what may arise from a respected she-teacher or a dangerous she-opponent. We will thus be able, in next § I-5 to speak of Óðinn's masculine magic in a softened context avoiding an implicit or hidden fight against feminine magic.

This gender problem raises two questions. The first one is to choose, in Hávamál 84 stating "*brigð* in their chest is lying", what exact meaning

Óðinn gives to the feminine noun 'brigð'? It would then be a 'simple' question of vocabulary.

The second one: "Is it (still according to Óðinn) in the 'nature' of women to be 'brigð'—whatever the meaning of that word?" It is a complex question related to women's örlög or to *sköp* practiced on all women by social forces eager to 'bewitch' them.

I-4.1. Are women, according to Óðinn, fickle?

The exact meaning of substantive 'brigð' in stanza 84 is clarified by the use that Óðinn does of the adjective 'brigðr' in s. 91. The Norse poets were masters of ON language who certainly could not confuse the meaning of the adjectival form and the substantive form of the same root—when they were known to have different meanings. Here are the relevant lines of the poem:

s. 84: "*brigðr* í brjóst of lagið"   controversy/breach in (their) breast
                                      is lying down.
s. 91: "*brigð* er karla hugr konum"   fickle are men's spirit with women.

You see that *brigðr* is not here translated by 'fickleness' but by 'controversy-breach' ('challenge-split' would be also possible) whereas the translations 'fickleness' seems to be standard one. Here are some examples of famous translations. Instead of 'rupture, flexibility, change' that are also possible, they give: Bellows: 'fickle'; Dronke and Orchard: 'fickleness'; Boyer: 'inconstancy', Larrington: 'deceit'. As a result, all these translators do not frown when implicitly stating that, for Óðinn, women are fickle or deceitful. These wordings are explicit insults addressed to women, they indeed are possible ones, which have unfortunately been adopted as 'obvious' by most academic translators.

However, the etymological dictionary of deVries gives for brigð: '*veränderung*' (change, modification), '*wankelmut*' (versatility) and '*lösungsrecht*' (right of cancellation). Why not to say that 'the right of cancellation' is 'lying in women's breast?' At least, this avoids being insulting. Moreover, for the dictionaries that do the difference between *brigðr* (faithless, fickle) and *brigð* (deVries does not) the latter only means, for example in LexPoet: "*varius* (varied, nuanced), *mobilis* (mobile, flexible), *inconstans* (fickle, inconsistent)." And we realize that, while Óðinn obviously insults men in s. 91 because they are *brigð* (fickle) with women, on the contrary, he does not necessarily insult women for their supposed frivolity but leaves the way open to an understanding similar to the one used above, which says that "controversy/ breach" instead of frivolity is lying in their breast.

This argument may seem fragile when we observe the relative uncertainty of *brigð* translation from the strict point of view of vocabulary. This last objection might be locally true, though it is false in the general context of Hávamál. In stanzas 96–110, Óðinn will give us two examples of these supposedly '*brigð*' women. The one of Billings mær describes a cunning woman who cheated him by promising her body while she will offer him the one of her bitch. It cannot be said that Billings mær is 'fickle'. She is cunning and clever, even deceptive, excessively breaching, but we can observe in stanzas 98–102 that, with her own weapons, she mainly defends herself against Óðinn's insistence, a probably unwelcome one. The second example is the one of Gunnlöð where he describes a woman who accepted him, saved his life and whom he left for reasons he does not make explicit (we however know through other sources that he aims at bringing the mead of poetry to the god's home, Ásgarðr). In view of stanzas 104–108, we understand that Gunnlöð is "an excellent woman" (s.108) with whom Óðinn has indeed been fickle. In stanza 110, the poet comments on Óðinn's attitude in such a severe way that we wonder if Óðinn is not pleading guilty since he is ashamed by his behavior. In the broader context of the stanzas that follow s. 84, in between a cunning Billings mær and an excellent Gunnlöð, describing women as 'fickle' would be to accept that Hávamál poets themselves were also 'fickle' to their own thinking.

I-4.2. *Are women, according to Óðinn, <u>naturally</u> brigð (its meaning being sharp or fickle)?*

If women's disposition leads all of them to be *brigð*, this implies in an Old Norse vision of the world that all women's örlög contain a clause that states they show this feature. Norse örlög are not exactly identical to our 'fate': Norns's decrees are totally forceful and blindly followed. As a consequence all women should be 'brigð', whatever they may do to avoid it. This would imply a kind of uniformity of behaviors in the feminine gender which is simply contradicted by the multiplicity of their behaviors, and in particular by the two examples of Hávamál encountered in § 4-1, above.

In order to 'explain' this feminine trait, two other verses of s. 84 declare that

"því at hverfanda hvéli	"because on a rotating wheel
váru þeim hjörtu sköpuð."	were their hearts shaped."

Often, translators see '*sköpuð*' as the past participle of the verb 'to do'. Let us recall that it is the one of *skapa* (to shape) to which a magic role is often associated. In the poetic Edda, we meet nine instances of *sköpuð* and only one of them is possibly not tinged with magic. Therefore, we understand it as a verbal form meaning '(shaped) *sköp*', i.e. 'shapings', a magic that is allowed to gods and humans. Here, the poet probably uses an image similar to the one of a potter's wheel with which gods or humans magically include 'brigð-ness' in women's souls.

Again, we may be surprised that, a bit as in the fairy tale 'Sleeping Beauty', the magicians creating these *sköp* take care of each little girl at birth, as the fairies took care of the little princess, so that all women would be concerned. This evokes a kind of vast conspiracy of the parents and relatives of each female baby.

However, thinking it over, we must note that feminists are so often pointing at such a conspiracy led by our social environment, supposed to influence in one way the female part of our population and in another way its male share. Feminist movements, not without generating sneers, have often emphasized how the gender of children is unconsciously directed by their parents.

It is difficult for anyone to accept that one's own behavior is governed by one's unconscious. That is why we are going to examine a single particularly striking example of unconscious behavior that penalizes the female gender, at least among French speaking people. It is relative to teaching how grammatical gender of adjectives is chosen when they modify two substantives of different gender. French grammar, perhaps even based on conscious androcratic reasons dating back a few centuries (but this does not illustrate our case), decided that the modification should be made in accordance with the grammatically masculine noun. It was necessary to choose between the two genders, as far as grammar is intended to be normative (again, this does not illustrate our case). All French pupils knew that the way of expressing this grammatical rule, in the course of time, became: "masculine prevails over feminine" which made millions of French boys (including me) snigger when their teacher stated this rule. I also know that my grandmother who was a teacher and a feminist taught this rule from 1905 to 1941, not without some teeth-grinding, during her career.

This means that all elementary grammar teachers unconsciously participated in a sort of universal conspiracy, the effect of which was, in practice, to discredit feminine gender. You may have noticed that a few lines above, the same rule is given in a natural way, without including any hint pejorative to the feminine gender. There exist probably hundreds of different ways to do the same or better and yet "masculine trumps the feminine (*le masculin l'emporte sur le féminin*)" has remained the norm for more than a century, according to what I directly observed.

In this case, we cannot speak of a consciously fomented conspiracy against the feminine gender. On the other hand, the long-term adoption of the double meaning of this grammatical rule points at a kind of archetype of the male unconscious which impels men to humiliate women, especially if the will of humiliation can be concealed in joking, double meaning remarks, etc.

In this sense, the social environment indeed pushes all girls to accept implicit derogatory rules they will share, which generates more or less suffering depending on their disposition. The details vary from one civilization to another, whether with magic *sköp* or humiliating ways of speech, as stated by Óðinn, that: "their hearts are shaped on a turning wheel." All this tends to reduce the importance of womanliness in our civilizations.

However, the two lines of s. 84 in which Óðinn states that the "hearts of women are shaped on a turning wheel," have very different meanings whether we accept that women are fickle (inducing a pejorative context relative to them) or that they are prone to controversy/breach (inducing a more neutral context relative to them). In a pejorative context, Óðinn's statement looks as a *sköp*-like curse by which women cannot escape being fickle. In a neutral context, Óðinn does not launch *sköp* on the feminine gender, he rather states an objective fact, possibly an unfortunate one, valid in the ON civilization, namely that, as above said, they tend to dispute their conditions of life ('controversy') and, if they fail to convince they then tend to depart from the unconvinced averse party ('breach').

Finally, taking into account the two examples of women he presents, the one of Billings mær (who ridicules him) and Gunnlöð (whose life he destroys), enable us to understand Óðinn's view as follows: In ON civilization, Óðinn states that if a woman revolts against the constraints she suffers, she becomes 'automatically' a contentious woman as illustrated by Billings mær. If she cannot or will not rebel, then she will become a broken woman, as Gunnlöð underwent.

I-5. Yggdrasill seen as a provider of Óðinn's magic

In § I-3.2 we could understand why Yggdrasill can be viewed as a kind of open sanctuary in which magic flourishes. Now that some of the classical prejudices against Óðinn have been cleared in § I-4, we may speak of his magic without being hampered by some views of his magic being devilish or the like.

We know that Óðinn is associated to several magic items: the first is Mímir's head providing him wisdom, and four objects the best known of them are a chair wherefrom he can watch the whole word, a spear that flies over the enemy, a magic ring that generates new rings and a drink called skalds' mead or Óðrœrir that is kept in a container bearing the same name. He is also associated to several animals: his eight-legged horse, his two wolves, his two ravens. Aside from these 'complements' to Óðinn's personality, we know that he carries inside him a large amount of knowledge relative to magic. This knowledge is known for coming from two sources. One is *seiðr* (or *seið*) he learned from Freyja, the other one is the runes he learned while hanging on Yggdrasill.

His knowledge of *seiðr* is announced in Ynglinga Saga chapter 7, called Óðinn's Bewitchments, the first part of Snorri Sturluson's Heimskringla ([humankind's] Home-circle) also known under the name of 'History of the Norwegian Kings'.

Seiðr magic is announced in this book as follows:

"Óðinn knew of skills that help further and are called *seiðr* and by which he was able to know the people's örlög and allot outstanding events that make luckless or unhealthy those that have to die. He could also catch a person's intelligence or strength and deliver them to another person. This black magic (*fjölkynngi* underlined below), though, produces so much feminineness (**ergi**) that men had no mind to fare this track and pagan priestesses were allotted this skill."

Some readers may wish to observe how Snorri expressed these ideas: they find below a 'as strictly literal as possible translation' of the ON he used (in italics) where the equivalent English words are directly under the corresponding ON Norse one.

We followed Dillmann's (2006) advice to translate '*ergi*' by a word neuter to sexuality as 'feminineness'. In some cases, especially when *ergi* is used as an insult, this word does point at a male homosexual relation or female 'over-sexuality' but Dillmann notes other examples asking for a less strongly sexual understanding.

Óðinn kunni þá íþrótt   svo   að mestur máttur   fylgdi   og framdi sjálfur,
Óðinn knew of this skill which the greatest power that (self-)helped and furthered self,

---

er seiður heitir,   en af því   mátti hann   vita   örlög   manna
is *seiðr* is named, and by which had power him to know the örlög of human ones

---

*og óorðna   hluti svo,   og að gera   **mönnum bana***
and outstanding events he allotted thus, and make humans **mortal (or dead) ones**

---

eða óhamingju eða vanheilindi,
either luckless or unhealthy,

---

svo og   að taka frá   mönnum   vit   eða afl   og gefa öðrum.
thus and to grasp from human ones intelligence or strength and give to others.

En þessi   fjölkynngi,   er framið er,
But this bad knowledge (magic), is producer that

---

fylgir   svo   mikil   ergi   að   eigi þótti   karlmönnum skammlaust
follows thus much femininity   for   non thought   men   most shameless

---

við   að fara   og var   gyðjunum   kennd   sú íþrótt.
with   to fare   and were pagan priestesses 'knowledged' that skill.

It seems that putting great Óðinn 'All-father' in the position of being a goddess' faithful student should raise surprise. Let us hope that the lengthy argumentation of § I-4 convinced the reader that great god Óðinn's psyche was complex enough so as assimilating his debt to Freyja without any resentment.

Our civilization, as C. Jung describes it, produces all kind of psychic sicknesses due to the 'normally' antagonistic relations between our consciousness and our unconsciousness. As an answer to this unsecure state of mind, Jung suggests a necessary kind of assimilation of the conscious urges and the unconscious ones. He calls this process "Individuation" by which a human person may become un-divided, i.e. a genuine individual. Freyja's teachings to Óðinn may be understood as her helping him to reach his individuation.

Let us now look at the other feature of Óðinn's magic, i.e. runic magic as it is reported in Hávamál s. 138–141. A score of comments relative to their classical and less classical understandings is provided by the online commented translation of Hávamál (see bibliography).

These stanzas describe how Óðinn gathered his runic knowledge. Perhaps the most striking one is found in two lines of s. 138:

… *ok gefinn Óðni,*	and given to Óðinn,
sjalfur sjalfum mér…	self to 'self-mine'…

It underlines the idea that runic knowledge is not a straightforward way of thinking but a recursive one in which the magician has to become aware of the psychic fact that he/she is able to think about his/her thinking: it is requested from each magician that he/she should also be able to 'give him/her to him/herself', which again puts forward the necessity of some kind of 'individuation' as Jung calls it. As far as Jung (1995) tells it, individuation is a lengthy process and he himself claims to have reached it quite late in his life.

We unfortunately cannot find in ON literature a detailed description of the way magic has been taught though some individuals are said to teach runic magic to one or several pupils. The most detailed account relative to this process is given in Sigrdrífumál where Sigrdrífa teaches runic knowledge to Sigurðr. This evokes a parallel teaching to the one of Freyja, and the one of Yggdrasill when Óðinn was hanging on the "windy tree." Here, a prose commentary says that, among heroes of a status intermediate between a godly characters and plain human ones, the most powerful warrior of Germanic mythology humbly "asks her to teach wisdom, whether she had news from all the worlds."

I-6. Humankind's two weaknesses: *Örlöglauss ok lítt megandi*

We can notice that many people are a bit too proud of our gods' gifts. Here they are, presented in Völuspá s. 18:

önd *gaf Óðinn,*	**breath** gave Óðinn,
óð *gaf Hænir,*	**intelligence** gave Hænir,
lá *gaf Lóðurr*	'**sea**' (internal water) gave Lóðurr
oc **lito góða.**	and a **beautiful hue.**

We less often hear of what they have not been given, though stanza 17 clearly states:

fundu á landi	they found on the ground
lítt megandi	**little** having **might**
Ask ok Emblu	Ask (r) and Embla
Örlöglausa	**örlög-less** (deprived of örlög).

Megandi is a present participle of the verb *mega* that means 'to have the strength to act, to procure a benefit'.

Völuspá states first that the first human images had little might and were 'örlögless' which suggests that the gods refused to or were unable to provide humans with örlög and might. These two disabilities characterize beings who are only sketches of human beings before the gods give them the gifts of stanza 18. Thus, those who are not able to overcome this handicap, i.e. those who are unable of action and who have no örlög can be qualified as human-drafts. They are not subhuman ones, as some ideologies claim or imply, but maybe incomplete humans. We could say, after their death, nothing more than they never had succeeded becoming 'real' human beings.

Conversely, the gods' gifts, that is breath, intelligence and flowing blood, are attributed to all humans without exception and we cannot escape this fact. For example, all the miracles of modern medicine may be able to camouflage poor blood circulation, but those who received a damaged gift from the gods will have to adjust their way of living to 'do with' as bravely as possible.

This difference between given qualities and self-created qualities enables us to understand why Norse civilization developed two archetypes that have lost their strength in our civilization.

The first of these archetypes, the simplest to understand, is the one of 'capacity to act'. Since nothing limits us, only our environment can prevent the execution of certain actions. In the ancient Norse civilization, the importance of acting properly is underlined by the fact that in Hávamál, Óðinn's advice on how to manage our actions occupies about 60% of the stanzas. Our civilization is presently witnessing the damage caused by this feverishness to act on our environment. If we were able to reduce this feverishness by 40%—which fits the 40% spiritual life in Hávamál—we would probably be able to largely limit the damage … but our civilization seems to recklessly reject any decreasing of economic growth.

The second archetype is the one of 'odd' destinies called örlög by the Norsemen. It deeply differs from what we call 'fate' or 'destiny' or 'wyrd' in Anglo-Saxon times (see details in Appendix 1 below before chapter II). On the one hand, örlög are presented as being intangible: no one can escape one's örlög. On the other hand, it seems that Norse wizards put a remarkable amount of energy at creating shapings called *sköp* that, precisely, modify the 'destiny' (in the modern sense of the word) of some individuals without however being able to modify their örlög. The best explanation to this apparent contradiction is that örlög deal with extremely general constraints, the details of which are handled by *sköp*, that is to say by human magic, witchcraft. In other words, örlög do not decide of every detail of someone's fate, parts only of his/her fate are örlög bound. *Sköp*, that is witchcraft produced by human ones or by gods, kind of fill up the part of our fates that is not taken in charge by örlög.

This being, we must also note that Óðinn, in Hávamál stanza 56, uses an unexpected argument to advise wizards to avoid knowing too much of örlög. He says:

Meðalsnotr	Not over-much wise
skyli manna hverr;	should be each human being;
æva til snotr sé,	never (strive) towards wisdom,

<u>örlög sín</u>	his <u>örlög</u>
viti engi fyrir,	(do) not (stay) in front of the <u>wise one</u>
þeim er sorgalausastr sefi.	whose mind lacks the most of sadness.

In this translation, we make of <u>*viti*</u> (a leader), 'a leader in wisdom, a wise one', since line 3 refers to wisdom.

The poet uses a double negation to tell us, in the last line, that the 'leader in wisdom' who ignores his 'örlög before', that is to say his future, is also the one who misses the most of the spirit of sadness, that is, he is the most joyful one. Thus, Óðinn tells us that knowledge of future drops us into a spirit of sadness. This is one of the reasons why it is hard to believe that runes were created to read the future: Óðinn himself advises against this type of concern.

This stanza may suggest that ancient Scandinavian magicians perhaps flirted (a bit too much in Óðinn's view) with örlög but that they sought above all to create shapings, *sköp* that could influence some of their contemporaries' lives, though not their örlög. This is looked upon as black magic, hated by monotheists. The new magicians of our century are working on the destinies, in the current sense of this word, not on örlög, and those who use the runes, including modern 'rune masters', do so in a way adapted to the meaning of the word 'destiny' in our civilization.

To conclude, let's say first that it seems that we are *örlöglauss* for a good part of our life (say, for example, until adolescence crisis) which makes of us incomplete human beings in the ancient Norse worldview. This does not mean that we have to learn of our örlög but rather that, when örlög seem to manifest themselves, we have to carry them out, or to proudly suffer them because they are teaching us (often quite brutally) that we are 'real' human ones, also called "humankind's human ones" as does old knowledge.

I-7. A female heroic character: Brynhildr (formerly known as Sigrdrífa) as in poem 'Sigurðarkviða in skamma'

She is a character central to the magic of several poems and we will meet her again in Chapter II where we will provide details on her links with magic. For now, since herself and her relations with the hero Sigurðr has been so often fantasized, we will recall the information on her life as told by the poetic Edda.

She is a king's daughter who dreamed of a warrior's life and became a Valkyrie (dead warrior—chooser) named Sigrdrífa. She was thus in charge to bring Óðinn's chosen to his 'hall of the dead warriors', Valhöll. In this case, the choosing seems to have included a killing since she happened to refuse to bring back the warrior chosen by Óðinn, killing another warrior who seemed to her better suited to die.

In order to punish her, Óðinn prickled her with the 'sleeping thorn' (here seen as a special kind of *sköp*) that put her to sleep until a hero would dare to wake her up.

The Norns had visibly decided that this hero would be Sigurðr since several seers told him this episode of his örlög. She then taught him rune magic and they swore an undying love to each other.

They then joined the Franks' kingdom. There, Sigrdrífa's name has been changed into 'Brynhildr' who became the one by which she is best known. As a result of magic nasty tricks (well-known ones, but we now skip some details given later), the wife of the Frank's king (Gunnarr), caused Sigurðr forgetting the oaths he pledged to Brynhildr. As a consequence, Sigurðr married Gunnarr's sister Guðrún.

We will see in § I-12 that Gunnarr will plot the slaughter of Sigurðr who was sleeping near his wife Guðrún.

When Brynhildr learns that 'her' hero has been killed, she becomes mad with pain and insults the Norns she blames for her unhappy fate. She declares that these Norns 'cast a spell' on her and Sigurðr:

ljótar nornir	wretched Norns
skópu *oss langa þrá.*	**shaped** for us a lengthy painful yearning.

This use of *skapa* preterit can hardly carry a mundane meaning since this shaping is done by Norns and they shape Brynhildr's feelings.

By saying this, she equates the Norns with "wretched human witches," a quite heavy way of speech.

I-8. A male heroic character: Sigurðr avenges his father's murder

Here is an episode of Sigurðr's life which is perhaps less known than others because it looks like a digression in the hero's life. It is nevertheless a central episode of his life, describing how Sigurðr rebels against his mentor Reginn and prepares to escape the 'spells' (*sköp*) that Reginn has thrown at him. According to these *sköp*, Reginn was going to kill Sigurðr after the latter had killed the dragon Fáfnir and recovered the treasure that Reginn has for a long time coveted. It seems that many commentators, who are little interested in magic, did not understand this battle of magic between Sigurðr and Reginn and preferred to leave it aside.

In fact, the poem Reginsmál explicitly tells us about Reginn's plans. He declares that he will educate Sigurðr and boasts of creating a destiny (örlög) that will bind Sigurðr to him. This is explained in Reginsmál stanza 14, where Reginn declares that Sigurðr will become glorious and chained to örlög (the ones that he, Reginn, will have shaped by his magic):

Ek mun fæða	I will school
folkdjarfan gram	the angry lord (Sigurðr)
nú er Yngva konr	Yngvi's parent
með oss kominn;	comes with us;
sjá mun ræsir	he will be the leader
ríkstr und sólu;	most powerful under the sun;
rymr um öll long	glorious in all countries
<u>*Örlögsimu.*</u>	<u>Örlög-chained</u> (literally: "örlög-chains").

Thus, Reginn asserts his claim to write Sigurðr's örlög (no one but the Norns is allowed to write örlög and you guess he will pay this impudence).

Reginn wants to take Sigurðr to Fáfnir's cave with the aim of recovering the treasure Fáfnir had seized. However, Sigurðr haughtily refuses. It would be ridiculous for the prince to have more "the desire to look for red rings (of red gold) than for the revenge of his father!" They thus undergo to punish Sigurðr's father murderer. We may guess that Sigurðr is going to make short work of his father's murderer. But then a *munr* (particular moment or meaningful coincidence, called synchronicity by C. Jung) takes place. The meanings of word *munr* is fully described in the references 'Huginn and Muninn' as a base for understanding the role of Óðinn's ravens and the difference between Huginn (Intelligence) and Muninn (Passion).

This *munr* takes place when, 'simultaneously', Sigurðr gets rid of Reginn's influence and avenges his father's death. Following the ancient tradition, the only honorable punishment of a father's murderer is achieved by his son who has to apply the bloody eagle technique (severing the ribs in the back). After this ceremony, Sigurðr will have found back his warrior's honor and he becomes able to reject Reginn's influence.

Reginsmál stanza 26 says:

Nú er blóðugr örn	Now is the bloody eagle
bitrum hjörvi	with the biting sword
bana Sigmundar	for Sigmund's death [Sigurðr's father]
á baki ristinn.	on the back engraved.

This also tells us that these 'bloody eagles' are not a stupid torture (as we tend to believe) but a ceremony in which the offended orphan finds back his honor … and escapes those who raised him without true paternal love.

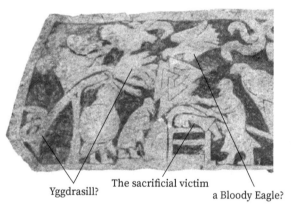

Yggdrasill?   The sacrificial victim   a Bloody Eagle?

Stora Hamars Stone, Sweden (Gotland island)

Seeing Yggdrasill in this image is far from being classical. Note however that its roots are quite 'serpent-like' and that an ordinary tree, just behind it, does not bend itself in order to participate in the ritual. Its top thus achieves the triplet of sacred symbols that consecrates the sacrifice: An Eagle, a Valknut and Yggdrasill.

In the poem Fáfnismál, after Sigurðr killed Fáfnir, 'spirits' in the form of these birds we call nuthatches, tell him that either Reginn will kill him or he will kill Reginn. Thus…

"Sigurðr hjó höfuð af Regin"   Sigurðr cut off Reginn's head

and found back his proper fate, the one that the Norns carved for him on wood chips, no longer the one planned by Reginn's *sköp*.

Appendix 1: Quotations and meaning of *wyrd* in Anglo-Saxon poetry

These quotations all belong to web available Anglo-Saxon (A-S) texts, they may be somewhat incomplete. The consulted translations looked so far from a literal translation that they have been restored, while keeping their basic meaning, as given by an A-S specialist. Word wyrd is presented in its context, together with a few words of the poem enabling to precise its particular meaning in this context.

These 21 citations state what is really known of wyrd, apart from the mass of literature they generated. Except the last two, they all belong to texts classed as 'pagan' because they do not cover biblical topics. The Christian God is nevertheless far from being ignored in them.

As we shall see, Heathen texts show some Christian influence but, symmetrically, even Christian texts do not completely forget their Heathen origins.

The dictionaries explain that the words *wyrd* (= fate in Anglo-Saxon) and *urðr* (= fate in Norse) are cognates, i.e. at some point in the past they have a common etymology. This is expressed by a strong linguistic link. Wyrd is related to verb *weorðan*, to become. The Norse word *urðr* is related to verb *verða*, to become, (*urðu* in its plural preterit = they became).

We cannot, however, identify wyrd and Norn *Urðr* since Norse tradition shows three different Norns: *Urðr, Verðandi* and *Skuld* who take in charge örlög, usually translated as 'fate, destiny'.

Beowulf

Line 455
Gæð a wyrd swa hio scel. Fare fate has it shall.

Line 475

wigheap gewanod;	the warriors disappear
hie wyrd forsweop	since wyrd swept them away
on Grendles gryre.	by Grendel's violence.

Line 572

Wyrd oft nereð	wyrd oft protects
unfægne eorl,	the non-doomed earl,
þonne his ellen deah.	when he is of courageous hue.

Line 734

Ne wæs þæt wyrd þa gen	Let wyrd prevent
þæt he ma moste	that he takes more
manna cynnes	men of the kin
ðicgean ofer þa niht.	often again after this night.

Line 1056

þone ðe Grendel ær	the one that Grendel already
mane acwealde	killed
swa he hyra ma wolde	and greedy he would kill others
nefne him witig god	if not the wise god
wyrd forstode	had protected their wyrd,
ond ðæs mannes mod.	and the man's (Beowulf) bold mood.

Line 1205

hyne wyrd fornam,	him wyrd destroyed
syþðan he for wlenco	when by arrogance,
wean ahsode,	he looked for danger,
fæhðe to Frysum	enmity to the Frisians.

Line 1233

Wyrd ne cuþon,	Wyrd they did not know,
geosceaft grimme,	fate grim,
swa hit agangen wearð	that they possessed would
eorla manegum,	the many earls
syþðan æfen cwom	when the evening comes.

Note: *geosceaft* means also 'fate'.

Line 1526

ac unc furður sceal	such further shall
weorðan æt wealle,	become near the wall,
swa unc wyrd geteoð,	such wyrd has settled,
metod manna gehwæs.	fate of humankind everywhere.

v 2040

wyrd ungemete neah	wyrd excessively near
se ðone gomelan	then the aged

gretan sceolde,	to approach shall,
secean sawle hord,	seize the soul's hoard,
sundur gedælan	sunder to pieces
lif wið lice,	life with body,

Line 2575

swa him wyrd ne gescraf	thus to him wyrd not allotted
hreð æt hilde.	victory at war.

Line 2814

Ealle wyrd forsweop	all the wyrd swept away
mine magas	my family
to metodsceafte,	to their fate-building,
eorlas on elne	earls in their courage.

Note: *metodsceaft* = fate-construction, doom.

The Wanderer

Line 5

Wyrd bið ful aræd!	Wyrd will be fully resolute!

Line 15

Ne mæg werig mod	Not may weary mood
wyrde wiðstondan,	wyrd withstand,
ne se hreo hyge	nor does scabby heart
helpe gefremman.	help bring.

Line 100

wæpen wælgifru,	the weapons death-givers,
wyrd seo mære,	wyrd famous,
ond þas stanhleoþu	and those cliffy stones
stormas cnyssað,	storms strike,

The Seafarer

Wyrd biþ swiþre,	Wyrd is stronger
Meotud meahtigra,	God mightier
þonne ænges monnes gehygd.	than any man could think.

Maxims 2

Line 5

wyrd byð swiðost, winter byð cealdost.	wyrd is the strongest, winter the coldest.

The Ruin

Line 24

Beorht wæron burgræced,	Shiny was the fortress,
burnsele monige,	bathes many,
heah horngestreon,	haughty the abundance of pinnacles,
heresweg micel,	martial sounds many,
meodoheall monig	the mead-hall many
dreama full,	of joy full,
oþþæt þæt onwende	until this moved
wyrd seo swiþe	wyrd this swept away.

The Rhyming Poem

Line 70

Me þæt wyrd gewæf,	For me what wyrd spun,
ond gewyrht forgeaf,	and my deeds brought,
þæt ic grofe græf,	is that I a trench dig,

Dream of the road

Line 74

þa us man fyllan ongan	then the men to cut down began
ealle to eorðan.	all to the earth.
þæt wæs egeslic wyrd!	Was that a horrible wyrd!

Follow now two examples of purely Christian texts that use the word wyrd.

Part of Exodus called The Crossing of the Red Sea

Line 458

ne ðær ænig becwom	not one came back
herges to hame,	of the warriors at home,
ac behindan beleac	but locked behind
wyrd mid wæge.	by wyrd among the waves.
þær ær wegas lagon,	Where was a way laying,
mere modgode,	the sea became furious
mægen wæs adrenced.	the army was drowned.

Life of St Guthlac

Line 1351

þroht þeodengedal,	suffering God-separation
þonne seo þrag cymeð,	when that times comes
wefen wyrdstafum.	spun by the wyrd-staff.

Note: *stæf* mean 'stick, staff', *wyrdstafum* = with wyrd's stick.

Comments

These examples show that the concept of wyrd has been assimilated by A-S Christianity, i.e. by Christians still born among Heathen concepts: for instance, the Jews are saved because the Egyptian warriors have got a 'bad' wyrd. This would be deemed today as being slightly iconoclastic. Worse, St Guthlac's wyrd is what cuts the connection between him and his lord God!

Conversely, it is also obvious that Heathen poems show some influence from a Christian way of thinking, which carries also a Roman influence. Even though the *witig god* in Beowulf's line 1056 could well be Heathen god, The Navigator's *Meotud* (= fate, God, Christ) almost certainly is the Christian God. However, again here, paralleling God's and wyrd powers is iconoclastic.

The power of wyrd is described as being huge, it sweeps away, overpowers, allots, grants, it secretly makes ready to strike us, it is *egeslic* and *mære*, that is: terrible and famous or 'great' [sometimes translated as 'inexorable' in online versions.].

We also note that its features vary from text to text in an incoherent way.

For example, often wyrd cannot be at all opposed in Beowulf line 1526 saying that it is "fate of humankind everywhere" or line 5 of The Wanderer telling that "Wyrd will be fully resolute" and this meaning is implied in many instances.

Its absolute power is nevertheless several times disputed. In Beowulf line 572 "the earl of courageous hue" is protected by wyrd, implying that courage may accommodate wyrd; line 1205 announces a rational cause supporting wyrd; The Wanderer, line 15, states that a scabby heart nor a weary mood "may withstand" wyrd (implying that the opposed dispositions might better resist); line 70 of the Rhyming Poem says that wyrd and our deeds both lead us to death (supposing that 'trench' is here a grave), that our duty is to 'cooperate' with wyrd.

We finally observe the idea that human ones are partially responsible for their destiny, which is well summarized by the Christian formula: "God helps who help themselves." This points at some 'modern minded' influence that swells in the present civilization where each one believes he/she can drive her/his own destiny.

Another influence, that one of Heathen origin, is a partial assimilation of wyrd to Latin Parcae. For example, both, Rhyming Poem and Life of St Guthlac say that wyrd spun the hero's life. We see in these ways of speech an instance of the practice describing our destiny as woven by wyrd. This practice is thus justified, for wyrd, by very old ways of speech. In studying ON örlög, we will see that this weaving has nothing to do with Heathen Germanic mythology: the Norns do not spin the örlög, they carve it on "wooden tablets." (see § II-1.4).

CHAPTER II

Digging Out Magic Behaviors and the Relationships Among Them

This chapter studies a list of Poetic Edda poems that contain a word related to magic. This provides the context in which the 'magic' words occur and enable the reader to decide by him/herself if this context really alludes to magic. When necessary, the meaning of the stanza receives itself a comment that put the stanza in context within the whole poem or with the whole of Norse mythology.

II-1. Destiny in Völuspá: stanzas 17–20 and 31, then 2, 46 (on *miöt*, measure)

An online commented translation of Völuspá is available See bibliography.

II-1.1. *Humankind and its destiny*

Völuspá, that will be supplemented by Hávamál, describes the fundamental components of humankind: what defines a human being? We find an answer in Völuspá stanzas 17, 18 and 20.

First of all, let us stress that stanza 17 speaks of a human couple, Ask and Embla, who are not yet a man and a woman, because they still miss two features to belong to humankind. Let us stress that these features are common to men and women. This forever splits old Germanic spirituality from the one of all the cultures in which the gods differentiate man and woman while bringing them into humankind either in a specific ordering, or showing different qualities.[3]

Before going into details, let us consider another general trait of these human features. Stanzas 17 and 18 describe five non-human inabilities, two in stanza 17, three in stanza 18. The two incapacities of stanza 17 will not be cancelled by a 'godly gift'. Conversely, the gods will gift humankind with the capacities described at the beginning of stanza 18.

The two deficiencies described in stanza 17 are to be *lítt megandi*, i.e. 'having little strength to act' (i.e. weak and inactive) and being '*örlöglauss*', without destiny. It thus seems that it is up to mankind to manage to acquire strength for acting and destiny. [We will soon refine this statement.]

The three godly gifts, quoted in stanza 18 are: *önd*, breath, *óðr*, intelligence and *lá*, properly 'the sea along the shores', a rather obvious image of internal water, blood, lymph and cell waters, which we will call here 'life force' and 'joy of life', and that gives also a beautiful color to human faces, as stated by stanza 18. In other words, breath, intelligence and life force/joy are gods' gifts and they should be enough for humankind to find the means of creating its own capacity of action and its destiny. Note that this interpretation exactly matches the modern belief of being able of "self-forging our destiny."

However, this incredibly modern point of view, found in stanzas 17 and 18, must immediately be moderated by an information given later, in s. 20.

---

[3] It is interesting to compare, from this point of view, the Scandinavian myth with one of the Sumerian myths of humankind's creation. The great Sumerian god Enki quarrels with Ninhursaja, his wife, because she grew eight plants the destiny of which he did not ascertain. He hastens to do so and Ninhursaja is furious at the destiny inflicted to her plants—they will be used as food, which she did not wish. She curses Enki who then sickens and suffers in eight parts of his body. The clash is then settled by a crafty fox conciliator and Ninhursaja starts tending Enki's diseases. Associated to Enki's recovery and from his eight diseases are born eight children, gods or goddesses. The first two children and the last one are male and the five others seem to be female. While Enki's ribs are looked after, Ninhursaja gives birth to a seventh child, a goddess, Ninti the future "goddess of the month."

In this Sumerian myth, going back to at least 5000 years, beings of the two sexes are created in sequence and we easily observe, without being able to know why, that men begin and close the procedure.

This stanza teaches us that three Norns decide of human destinies by 'scraping wood tablets' i.e. by carving runes, as we soon shall see in § II-1.4. There is a compelling aspect in a destiny decided by higher powers, and this contradicts the above interpretation, a voluntarily hasty one. The topic of örlög is thus more complex than stanzas 17 and 18 suggested.

To have a destiny is certainly a fundamental component of human life though it opposes our need for freedom. For better understanding stanza 17 meaning, we should reconsider the relation between our capacity to act and örlög. The capacity to act opens the doors to freedom whereas örlög tends to shut them. If we state that rebelling against our destiny is, to some extent, forsaking our human statute, it should at once be recalled that the first human capacity, the one of acting, relentlessly moderates destiny.

In order to manage this knot of contradictions, we are driven to the following conclusion: It seems that a 'human destiny' is wedged between an inexorable destiny and a capacity for acting. Therefore, human ones cannot do more than their best! Despite everything, the capacity to act provides us with the possibility of discovering hints of our own destiny instead of blindly undergoing it. Once we will have acknowledged and understood our destiny, it will not any more appear absurd to us and we will be able to heartily achieve (or undergo) it. This is how we may understand the message sent by the völva to humankind.

As we already observed, örlög and destinies are quite complex topics. In order to deal with them, during the course of the book, we will meet quite a number of (unexpected?) references to the works of C. G. Jung (with a chapter 4 more or less structured by his ideas) because, as we shall see, several features of Old Norse spirituality express a strong relationship we could describe as a somewhat primitive—though quite complex—individuation process. The fight between "an inexorable destiny and a capacity for acting" is quite reminiscent of the 'competition' between unconscious urges and conscious wishes that create our psychic energy as described in Jung's 1st chapter of "The Structure and Dynamics of the Psyche," second edition (2014), in section 'The psychological Concept of Energy', pp. 14–18.

Let us now see what deeper understanding of these Völuspá stanzas we can reach.

The gods gifted us with three capacities.

The first, Óðinn's gift, is breath. We should never forget the obvious mechanical process such that the shape and disposition of our ribs makes it possible that our lungs would fill up with air. This is for the bodily point of view. Beyond that, though, breath enables us to identify with the forces of air (or celestial forces) and also to have "a lot of breath" that is to say, to find both inspiration and guts to carry on a difficult task.

The second, Hœnir's gift, is intelligence. From the bodily point of view, it is born in our brain (or also, for some, in our heart or our entrails) and it should not be forgotten that this faculty, of which human ones seem to be so proud, finds its source in one part of our body. In addition, it is obviously the faculty for proper thinking, for placing ourselves in space and time and for behaving rationally. Intelligence is also the partner of courage to give us reasons to continue a complex task, that may even become pleasurable because it titillates our intelligence.

The third, Lóðurr's gift, is 'the sea along the shore', i.e. the water of our body which ensures its functioning and which constitutes the greatest part of it. Here again, the material aspects of water should not be neglected. But it is also what puts us in contact, as the sea waves that break on the beach, with the combined forces of water and ground, which is a quite complete image of the forces of earth. In addition, these internal waters are the paramount source of life force and joy and of mankind's "beautiful hue", as pointed out by s. 18 last line as an expression of our zest for life.

Now, we can perhaps a little better understand why the gods did not judge propitious to provide us an örlög nor a specific capacity of action.

Let us combine courage, intelligence and joy in life and we will obtain a particularly effective way to motivate us to act "as it is necessary" i.e. without gloom, stupidity nor despondency. Discouragement is often the cause of our failures and joy in life helps us not to give up in front of the more overwhelming problems, otherwise "rather commit suicide" would be an obvious solution to all problems.

The case of örlög is more complicated to analyze. It seems that the gods did not want to take care of our örlög because they well knew that this topic belongs to the Norns and, in the ON religion, gods themselves are exposed to a destiny.

But they also knew that Norns do not deal with 'small details' of our lives. It is known that Norns are "the world's Hamingjur"[4] and they determine only a broad outline of our small individual destinies.

We will not escape, for example, from a global climatic warming which seems to belong to humankind's örlög. As seen in § I-1, there exist many global reactions to be opposed to a catastrophic reheating and many individual ones for living this reheating. All these reactions, if they make use of a certain form of magic, that could be called '*sköp*', conceived beside örlög. Each one of these sköp constitutes a particular way to live climatic reheating. This depends indeed on the courage, intelligence, life strength and joy in life of present time humankind, although we are inexorably subjected to humankind's destiny.

Some deny the existence of destiny, others are blindly subjected to it. Both standpoints deny the higher forces driving us or our gods' gifts. They are two parallel roads leading to a personal and social disaster.

II-1.2. Stanzas 17–18: Of gods and humankind

Völva's account is cut at stanza 9 by a succession of 7 stanzas giving the list of Dwarves' names. This account starts again at s. 17. At this point, it may be useful to consult our translation of Völuspá in order to put this stanza in its context.

---

[4] This way of speaking is given by CV at the word *Hamingja*. It probably results from an interpretation of the two occurrences of this word in poetic Edda, namely in Vafþrúðnismál s. 49 and Vegtamskvida (Baldr's dream) a stanza known as 'd' in Bugge's edition. A Hamingja is a protective spirit (the word hamingja means also 'luck') that sticks to certain individuals of a clan in order to protect the clan. The stanzas a-d are not often translated. Here is first half of 'd':

Baldr's premonitory dreams throw the Æsir into a panic, and all omens confirm that Baldr should soon die. Then the 'd' stanza starts as follows:

Valföðr uggir,	*van sé tekit,*	*hamingjur ætlar*	*horfnar mundu;*
Father of Death suspects	**lack is obtained,**	**haminjur he thinks**	**disappeared may;**
(Óðinn suspects that)	(there is a 'lack')	(he thinks the hamingjur)	(may have disappeared);

In other words, the situation appears to him as being hopeless, due to Hamingjur's disappearance.

Everything happened as described in stanzas 1–8, until…

Stanza 17:

Unz þrír kvámu	1.	Until three came
ór því liði	2.	out of their people (family place)
öflgir ok ástkir	3.	strong-always and loving-always
æsir at húsi,	4.	*æsir* to (mankind's) house,
fundu á landi	5.	they found on the ground
lítt megandi	6.	**little having might**
Ask ok Emblu	7.	Ask(r) and Embla
örlöglausa.	8.	**örlög-less** (deprived of örlög).

Comments on the vocabulary

Line 5: The word *land* describes the ground as opposed to the sea: 'where the sea stops'.

Line 7: The names of the first two human ones are here in the accusative (direct object of 'found'). We can read the man's name as Ask or Askr, identical in the accusative case. Askr means ash-tree but the experts sought in vain a tree name (or anything else) corresponding to Embla. Some translators wanted to attribute to her a tree name according to their personal beliefs. A modern-traditional example is the one of 'vine shoot' conveniently evoking a vine finding support on the solid ash, image of a fragile woman leaning on her strong man. All this is ridiculous, as well, from the point of view of the name 'Embla'.

Comment on the meaning of the stanza

Honesty however forces us to notice that the end of Völuspá s. 17 tells of a man named *Ask* and we will soon see that s. 19 beginning tells that Yggdrasill is also an '*askr*', which gives to male Norse persons some right to be looked upon as a support post. Indeed, if we examine the structure of the ancient Icelandic society as it is described by sagas, it seems that man is the (sometimes disputed) support in the external world whereas woman is the (undisputed) support of an inner world represented by the family dwelling. Conversely, this structure of the ancient Norse society is now seriously put in doubt … see Marianne Moen thesis (2019) and her extensive bibliography (Facebook group 'the Magic of Yggdrasill' has been created to favor discussions on such topics).

This stanza gives us also three valuable indications on what defines a 'real' human person.

Firstly, Ask and Embla are found both together and we will see that all positive features the gods will allot to them, in stanza 18, are given to both, without reference to gender, as already announced in § II-1.1 This stanza thus describes what misses in the primitive Ask and Embla for them being fully humans.

Secondly, they are both '*lítt megandi*' i.e. 'being only little able', unable to act. A fundamental quality of humankind is thus to be able of acting on the world.

Thirdly, they are both '*örlöglauss*', without destiny. The second fundamental feature in the definition of humankind is to be carried by their örlög. In the Anglo-Saxon literature *wyrd*, destiny, is invariably presented as an unbearable <u>outside</u> constraint (see first chapter appendix 1) whereas here, constraint or not, it is one of the two <u>inside</u> paramount features of human beings. To rebel against our örlög is to some extent thus seen as leaving our human status.

Moreover, the first god's gift, the one of acting, moderates fate's inexorability. As already suggested in § II-1.1, our human condition is to be wedged between our inexorable <u>inborn and unconscious</u> destiny and our <u>inborn and conscious</u> capacity to act. In other words, this tells that our psychic being includes, among others, two different parts, one belonging to our conscious psyche, capacity to act, and the other belonging to our unconscious psyche, örlög.

Stanza 18

Önd þau né átto,	Breath they did not own,
óð þau né höfðo,	intelligence they did not have
lá né læti	'the sea' [**internal waters**] does not flow
né lito góða;	nor (shows) a hue good (beautiful);
önd gaf Óðinn,	breath gave Óðinn
óð gaf Hænir,	intelligence gave Hœnir
lá gaf Lóðurr	'sea' gave Lóðurr
oc lito góða.	and hue beautiful.

This stanza does not explicitly speak of örlög but it shapes the general structure of a human being who does not exist without his/her örlög.

II-1.3. *Stanza 19: Yggdrasill*

ON	**Textually**
Ask *veit ek standa,*	**An ash-tree** I know rises,
heitir **Yggdrasill,**	it is called **Yggdrasill,**
hár baðmr, ausinn	raised <u>tree</u>, splashed
hvíta auri;	of white mud;
þaðan koma **döggvar**	from there comes **the dews**
þærs í dala falla,	that in the valley fall,
stendur æ to yfir grænn	always stands up above green [green, it stands...]
Urðar brunni.	Urðr' source.

Comment on the vocabulary

Askr, here in the accusative, ***ask***, means an ash-tree. The saying 'askr Yggdrasill' appears several times in Norse literature. This is why almost everyone claims that the tree of the Norse world is an ash-tree ... with the modern meaning of the word, *Fraxinus excelsior*. This is a typical anachronism and we may suspect that the only goal of the 'ash-tree-fanatics' is to introduce yet another contradiction in our mythology: Everyone knows that an "always green ash-tree" does not exist. In skaldic poetry, a classical technique is the one of using *heiti*, i.e. replacing the name of an object by another of similar meaning. For example, stating 'ash-tree' instead of 'tree'. There even exist lists of *heiti* that indicate which replacements were successfully used by the old poets. For example, the *heiti* for a tree ("*viðar heiti*") contains the word *askr*. It means that a traditional way to speak uses the word 'ash' to speak of a 'tree'. In this list of *heiti*, we find also the words *sverða, skipa, hesta* (sword, boat, horse) which could express the word *tree*, according to the context. (Source: Jónsson, Skjaldedigtning B1, downloadable at http://www. septentrionalia. net/etexts/skjald_b1.pdf).

Here, the word ***baðmr*** in the third line provides a context pointing at a tree.

Yggdrasill breaks up into *yggr* = fear and *drasill* (or *drösull*) = horse (exclusively in poetry).

– On *yggr*. The word *yggr* does not appear in CV that gives only *ýgr* = wild. It is found in deVries that associates it to *uggr* = fear. It is also given by LexPoet that identifies it with *ýgr*. The last two dictionaries announce that Yggr is one of the traditional names of Óðinn, which CV does also but not at the word *ýgr*.

— On *drasill*. The three dictionaries we use here provide the words *drasill* and *drösull* with this spelling. The spelling 'Yggdrasil' is how translators write it, avoiding to write the letter marking the nominative, here the second 'l'.

Döggvar = old plural nominative and genitive of *dögg*, dew.

Comment on the meaning of the stanza

Lines 3–6 describe a way of explaining why dew can settle on grass even from an uncloudy sky. By its roots, Yggdrasill is the support of all the Chthonian forces, including Niðhöggr, a 'dragon' living among Yggdrasill's roots. It can be called 'bottom snake' if we read 'nið', or 'slander snake' if we read 'níð' since *níð*, slandering, and *niðr*, a son or 'at the bottom', have very different meanings.

By its trunk, its higher roots and its lower branches, it is the support of the nine inhabited worlds.

By its high branches and its leaves, it is the carrier of all heavenly forces. The atmosphere, with or without clouds, contains some amount of moisture that settles in dew. The allegory contained in lines 3–6 is thus explained. It nevertheless could also bear a more mystical meaning, namely that the trees pour down a life source that flows upon our world.

II-1.4. Stanza 20: Norns

s. 20

Þaðan koma meyja	1. From there come maids
margs vitandi	2. much knowing
þrjár ór þeim sæ/sal,	3. three out of their sea/hall
er und polli stendr;	4. which below a pine stands;
Urð *hétu eina,*	5. **Urðr** is called one,
aðra Verðandi,	6. the other **Verðandi,**
–skáru á skíði,–	7. –they scraped <u>on</u> a wooden tablet—(12) ("the örlög of humankind" as in 12 with *seggja*=humankind's)

(örlög seggja, line 12)

Skuld *ina þriðju.*	8. **Skuld** the third one.
Þær lög lögðu,	9. They fixed the laws
þær líf kuru	10. lives they chose
alda börnum,	11. of humankind's children,
örlög seggja [or *segja?*]	12. örlög of-human-ones [*or* örlög they say].

Norns' names

The Norn's names are given in a special order which is certainly significant since the poem specifies that Urðr "is the one" and Skuld "is the third."

The word *urðr* is one of the Norse words meaning 'fate', as *örlög* and *sköp* among others. Due to the high frequency of "spinning of the wyrd" on the world web, we should be weary of possible Latin-Greek influences through Parcae's/Moirai's roles (more details have been provided in § I-1). This kind of misunderstanding is unavoidable since all translators are educated persons whose culture has been influenced by the Greek and Latin civilizations. Because of the meaning of the plural preterit of *verða*, *urðu* (they became), we can suppose that Urðr is somewhat linked to what happened in the past. Since the Norns do not deal only with individual destinies, we must understand that this 'past' actually is the sum of what happened to humankind, including our genetic inheritance, and even more generally the result of the whole evolution of our universe.

Verðandi is related to verb *verða*, now in its present participle tense, thus meaning 'becoming'. Here, there exists no real link with time since 'becoming' is an action that takes some time to occur and the claim she is the Norn of present time looks like a kind of cheating. Present time is a nice grammatical category but its semantics are almost empty since it has, so to say, a foot in our past and the other foot in our future. Verðandi is the Norn of what is undergoing a transformation and she may be seen as the Norn of evolution and action.

The word *skuld* means a debt, i.e. a commitment that cannot be avoided. When the saga or poetry characters complain of the unavoidable fate decided by the Norns, they essentially refer to Skuld. This name is also associated to a verb, *skulu* (shall and they shall). Its preterit is *skyldi*. It thus seems that Skuld could be associated to a sort of mix of a present and a past, which starts being absurd. It very clearly does not refer to any fixed period of time, and this confirms the doubts that time-based academic categorizations would apply at all to the Norns.

As announced, the ordering of the three Norns in s. 20 should be significant and, as already stated, we may be weary of an order based on time, namely past, present and future. Let us instead propose an ordering such that each Norn plays a specific role, based on logical relationships between them, while each is active in all three segments of grammatical time.

The above analysis of name Urðr suggests someone who, as a conscientious doctor provides a complete check-up, or as a financial controller provides an audit on the state of affairs. We could thus qualify her as being a **controlling authority**, who builds up a statement of accounts describing how humankind, and also individuals, have been, are, and will be managing their existence.

The role of Verðandi is easier to grasp, she is the **active authority** who decides on the way all actors of our universe have behaved, behave and will behave in view of the account provided by Urðr.

Skuld's name tells of her role: she evaluates the debts, and, with Verðandi's help, sees that these are refunded. We could thus call her a **"refunding authority."**

It is understood that these three activities cooperate among them along the line of time. The order met in s. 20 can be understood as a measure of the amount of direct constraint their decisions wield on people, even though each of them is not easy to counter.

Controlling asks for no more action than being aware of what has been happening.

Acting with efficiency implies a kind of common agreement between the leading authority and the many actors who are involved.

When mistakes have been done, the refunding authority, Skuld, is in charge of forcing on the actors what and how they should (*skyldi*) repay, like it or not.

We should notice that Norns' names and tasks may be interpreted in such a way they have some relationship with the ones of the Parcae and the Moirai. The main task of the last ones, however, is clearly devoted to the handling of individual fates. The Norn's tasks include the ones of their Greek and Latin counterpart and they besides deal with the fate of the gods and of the world.

Comments on the vocabulary and the structure of the stanza

The verb **skára** points at the action of mowing, which is not at all adapted to the context. The experts read *skara*, which means to scrape/poke and *skaru* gives 'they scraped'. The ON grammatical use of verb *skara* is similar to that of the English language, someone '*skarar*' an inscription (direct object—called here 'accusative') on a support (indirect object—called here 'dative'). You see that in line 7 the verb is followed with a dative (*skíði*) and it carries no accusative, it thus does not specify what the Norns *skara*.

We must also note that line 7 cuts the list of the names of Norns in an almost 'rude' way, where from comes the pair of—added by the editors of the poem. A detailed explanation is provided below.

The preposition **á** followed by a dative means on/upon. Since most translators do not read line 12 just after line 7, they tend also to forget to translate this slightly useless 'upon', in their understanding of these lines. They thus render the unambiguous dative *skíði* by an accusative: "they scrape wooden tablets."

The last line has always given serious trouble to the translators.

This **'seggja'** can be read as the verb *segja* (to say). With this last choice, örlög is an accusative related to this verb. It can also be read, as chosen here, as *seggja*, which makes of it the genitive plural of *seggr*, a messenger (who indeed 'says' something) and, in poetry, a human person. The choice between the two understandings is complicated because we know that the Middle Ages copyists themselves hesitated: There are two manuscripts (Codex Regius and Hauksbók) the first of which gives '*seggja*' and the second one '*at segja*'. This dilemma has been definitively solved by Elizabeth Jackson (1999—see bibliography). She proposes an elegant solution as follows: "The present article will argue, first, that the verb for line 12 is provided in line 7...)". This solution consists in keeping *seggja* and reading line 12 just after line 7: **skáru á skíði/örlög seggja** (they scraped on a wooden tablet/the örlög of humankind). This amounts to note that the missing accusative in line 7 is provided in line 12. This kind of 'jump' is not very frequent in Eddic poetry, though it is frequent in Skaldic poetry. Note a significant difference between the two versions. If Norns *segja* (state) örlög, any contending person may conclude: "they only state, therefore someone else allots these örlög." Jackson's interpretation makes it clear that the Norns are the ones who allot humankind's örlög.

Ek sá Baldri,	I <u>looked</u> at <u>Baldr</u>
blóðgum tívur,	blood-covered *divine being,*
Óðins barni,	(by) Óðinn's son,
örlög *fólgin;*	(I saw) **örlög** <u>hidden</u>;
stóð of vaxinn	was standing (fully) grown
völlum hæri	in the fields <u>taller</u>
mjór ok mjög fagr	slender and very beautiful
mistilteinn.	mistletoe.

II-1.5. Stanza 31: Baldr

Comment on the vocabulary

Verb *sjá*, to see, gives **sá** in its preterit first person. The name of god Baldr is in the dative case so that we must read verb *sá á* (to 'see on' = to look at). This meaning will be kept in the two following lines. In line 4, örlög is in the accusative case, we must thus understand '*sá*' alone and the völva says that she saw his hidden örlög.

The declension of *tívi* as *tívur* is somewhat irregular. This word is used in general in the plural and its dative is 'normally' *tívum*. Dronke tries to find an explanation to this variation and says that she failed finding a convincing one … I'll certainly not do better than her!

Verb *fela* means to hide, confuse/entrust, its past participle is ***fólginn***.

Adjective *hár*, high, does *hæri* in the comparative. Mistletoe is taller than the other trees or plants.

Comment on the meaning of the stanza

After being run through by Höðr's arrow, Baldr's corpse has certainly been covered with blood. If we try to see an allusion here, our only reasonable choice is to think of Óðinn, wounded by a spear while hanging and alive on the world tree. He had also to be blood-covered, as hinted at in Hávamál stanza 138. In addition, it seems that the warriors who did not die in combat could nevertheless join Óðinn in Valhöll by being 'marked' with "Óðinn's sign" by a spear, another bloody process related to Óðinn.

Baldr's örlög is hidden as everyone's else. It however seems that Frigg and Óðinn were informed of everyone's örlög, as several times noted in Lokasenna. Since this stanza underlines this topic, it must mean that neither Frigg nor Óðinn were able to foresee their son's fate. We already

(Note 3 in § II-1.1) spoke of the gods' panic when they were aware of Baldr's imminent death: Óðinn has been afraid that Hamingjur—certainly those of the gods' clan—had left as long as such a disaster could occur. Baldr is the first to die within gods' family and we can easily imagine that his death announces that other Æsir could die as well. Baldr's death can thus be looked upon as the first signal of Ragnarök's arrival.

The last four lines further increase the feeling of 'end of a world' for the Æsir. One of the three 'actors' in their son's murder, mistletoe, is proudly standing on the fields, as if pointing out their ultimate mortality. It may have seemed that the Æsir had defeated the universal chaos forces, but chaos strikingly, though poetically, forces the Æsir to remember them, by means of a vigorous 'mistletoe' stalk.

We can assume that the name 'mistletoe' points at a mythical plant the botanical name of which is unknown, since it cannot "proudly stand in the fields." Celtic religions gave a mythical status to botanical mistletoe, it quite possible that Norse people chose this name to point at a magical tree.

II-1.6. Stanzas 2 and 46 (on mjöt, measurement)

These two stanzas deserve comments that are already given in the online translation of Völuspá. They are quoted here because they provide indications on the meaning of *mjötuðr*, aside from its classical translation of 'destiny'. Three other instances in poetic Edda use it with the possible meaning of 'destiny' as we will later see.

Stanza 2

ON	Literal translation	English
2. *Ec man iötna*	I remember the giants	I remember the giants
ár um borna,	in old times born,	in old times born,
þá er forðom mic	those who in the past me	those who in the past
fœdda höfðo;	nourished to someone adult;	nourished me to become an adult;
nío man ec heima,	nine remember I countries,	I remember nine countries,
nío íviði,	nine Giantesses (or ogresses)	nine Giantesses
miötvið *mæran*	the measure-master famous	and the famous **measure-master**
fyr mold neðan.	toward the ground under.	still under the ground.

This stanza uses the word *miöt-viðr* = measurement-tree. CV sees in this formulation a copyist errors as if the expression 'measurement-tree' did not have any meaning. We already, in § I-3.1, explained why this statement is obviously wrong: Quite to the contrary, here, the tree of measure can only be Yggdrasill, which is still growing under the ground. This indicates that the time evoked by this stanza is incredibly ancient … which explains the last line of the stanza. This way of speech allots a divine role to Yggdrasill since *miötuðr* was understood, at least within the Anglo-Saxon world, as the Christian God.

In stanza 46 below, Dronke very aptly translated *miötuðr* by "fate's measure." A complete explanation of this word cannot be provided before our conclusion to chapter II.

Stanza 46

ON	Literal translation	English
Leica Míms synir,	Play/Move about Mímir's sons,	Mímir's sons move about,
enn **miötuðr** kyndiz at ino gamla	and **measure ruler** burns at him (= when resounds) old	and the measure ruler burns while old Gjallahorn;
Giallarhorni;	Gjallahorn;	loudly resounds.
hátt blæss Heimdallr,	up blows Heimdall,	up blows Heimdall,
horn er á lopti,	the horn is aloft,	the horn is aloft,
mælir Óðinn	speaks Óðinn	Óðinn speaks
við Míms höfuð;	with Mímir's head;	with Mímir's head;

II-2. Hávamál stanzas relative to destiny: Stanzas 41, 53, 56, 15, 126 and 145, 59 and 141, then 84 and 98

An online commented translation of Hávamál is available see bibliography.

The great Hávamál poem (Háva-mál = High's-word) by its title announces that the god Óðinn speaks to us through the skalds who wrote this poem. It contains 164 stanzas, all of them more or less allude to destiny, in particular the 95 first ones that provide advice about properly carrying out one's life. We will now study those specifying the meaning of *örlög* for Óðinn, even if they do not use this word.

We will start with stanza 41 that provides a somewhat commonplace example where destiny is regarded as unavoidable and constraining, as it happens in most sagas and with Anglo-Saxon *wyrd*. Other stanzas give interesting precise details as we shall now see.

Stanza 53 provides an example of a use of the verb *verða* which should have drawn the specialists' attention. Even though its traditional meaning 'to become' is possible, the context rather hints at "being destined to" and, as if by chance, it is used here in its plural preterit '*urðu*', a reminder to Norn Urðr.

Stanza 56 is the single Hávamál stanza explicitly using word *örlög* and, together with stanza 15, it introduces an unexpected concept: the one of "non-sadness" linked to ignorance of one's own destiny, i.e. joy in life is associated to this unawareness.

Three other stanzas give guidance in order to improve one's destiny.

Stanza 126: in a hidden way, Óðinn advises to avoid influencing other people's destiny because it is a source of social rejection.

Stanza 59 introduces the importance of feeling motivated in our life, just as a modern coach could advise us. Self-care and avoiding insouciance are necessary if we wish to achieve our private goals.

Lastly, stanza 141 gives us a difficult to achieve rule of building a harmonious and creative destiny by being 'learned', that is educated in all things and especially in magic.

At this point, it might be useful to look at a 'fortune wheel' dating from Roman times, a Pompeian mosaic. It represents destiny and illustrates how much mixing destiny, chance and fortune's wheel was already common during Roman times. It shows a kind of structure based on the attributes of poverty (on the right), of royalty (on the left) and death (central cranium), supported by a butterfly and a wheel. The butterfly represents the soul of a dead person in this mythology. It is available at http://www.convivial-iteenflandre.org/index.php?option=com_content&view=article&id=259:2e-citation-latine-2009-cr-vinci-hals&catid=38:citation-et-uvre-dart

II-2.1. *Knowledge of one's destiny and life joy:*
   stanzas 56 and 15

s. 56

Not over-much wise
should be each human being,
never (striving) towards wisdom;
his **örlög**
(does) not (stay) in front of the wise one
whose mind lacks the most of sadness.

s. 15 (lines 4-5-6)

glad and happy
will (be) each man
until he **endures** his death.

The three first lines of s. 56 state that excess of wisdom is not desirable: we should not constantly look for wisdom. Last lines of 56 describe, in a complicated way, the state of mind of a wise one who does not know his/her destiny (because it is not "in front of him/her").

Modern society has this in common with old Scandinavian society that, in another stanza, Óðinn denounces alcoholism when it is not related to some inspiring poetical motivation. Abuse of wisdom is also denounced in s. 56 above, which nowadays is not looked upon as a possible shortcoming. Imagine that we, nowadays, meet as many wise people than alcohol addicts and that both features were equally ostracized! We should however insist again on the fact that in old Scandinavian civilization, 'wisdom' largely includes knowledge of magic. Such Óðinn's remark underlines the importance, undoubtedly excessive, that magicians brought into discovering their personal örlög.

We also know that Frigg and Óðinn knew örlög "of anything." To some extent, trying to know one's own destiny amounts to competing the gods, and this is the mark of an impertinence which, indeed, is not really advisable to simple human ones.

In addition, stanza 15 specifies that each one should enjoy a merry life. When comparing with s. 56, we become aware that s. 15 implicitly tells that wisdom should not be too much concerned with destiny. Óðinn explains that wisdom excess leads to the knowledge of one's own örlög and brings a "spirit of sadness." This supports the advice given by stanza 15 to lead a happy life. This also shows that s. 15 is not a minor stanza because it advises a form of happy unconcern. It rather is a deeply pagan stanza that rejects the concepts of austerity, of research of Christian holiness or Buddhist illumination, i.e. a spirituality by which people aspire to forsake the humble human needs relative to our "shameful basely bodily" cares.

II-2.2. On motivation: stanza 59

He will rise early
he who reaches poets (*or* gets hold of workforce)
and goes towards the conscience of his verse-making (his poetical works),
(he goes into) much delaying
who sleeps the whole morning,
under (the urge of) impulses half of fate (*or* wealth) (is won).

The meaning of this stanza is ambiguous as shows the above translation. All the words used can either evoke a 'business' or poetic work. Some translators chose the most prosaic version but we cannot imagine Óðinn being impassioned for the ways of becoming rich while he was impassioned for poetry. To recover the magic mead of poetry, he accepted risking his life, and even breaking a sacred oath, as explicitly stated by Hávamál stanza 110. Hávamál context thus evokes a poet who must feel moved by his poetic destiny if he wishes to fulfill it. There is no question of implying here that a 'businessman' would not deserve to have a destiny but that Óðinn was certainly much more interested by the poets than by the good managers of their fortune.

II-2.3. Rules of active magic: Stanza 144

Veistu hvé rísta skal?	Do you know how to carve and hack?
Veistu hvé ráða skal?	Do you know how to advise, contrive, rule and punish?
Veistu hvé fáa skal?	Do you know how to fetch, win and paint?
Veistu hvé freista skal?	Do you know how to try, tempt and test?
Veistu hvé biðja skal?	Do you know how to ask, try to get (and even) beg?

Veistu hvé blóta skal?	Do you know how to sacrifice to the gods?
Veistu hvé senda skal?	Do you know how to dispatch (and even) kill?
Veistu hvé sóa skal	Do you know how to 'over use' (possibly) up to wiping out and slaughter?

Each of the 8 verbs used in stanza 144 may carry several meanings that have been sometimes understood differently depending on the background of the dictionary author: prose texts for CV, etymology for deVries and poetry for LexPoet.

2.3.1. *rísta* means 'to gash, chop, scrape, skin, carve' (CV). Lex.

Poet adds the following meanings: *scindere* (to split), *fabricare* (to produce), *insculpere literas* (to carve letters) and deVries *ritzen* (to scratch). The general feeling provided by all these verbs is one of brutality, not the one of a careful and quiet engraving. This suggests that rune carving is performed in a state of mind nearer to Odinic fury than the one of a well-balanced mind.

Skírnir's behavior, in the skaldic poem 'Skírnir's Travel', is a good example of an increasing fury until he threatens Gerðr with destructive rune magic since she refuses to accept to marry Freyr. He carves them in a furious state of mind though he instantly calms down when Gerðr agrees to his proposal.

The same poem shows that when a sorcerer wishes to destroy the power of carved runes, he/she will *af-rísta* ('carve off') them, as Skírnir claims to be able to perform in case Gerðr accepts to marry Freyr.

2.3.2. *ráða* means 'to advise, decide, contrive, rule, explain, punish' (CV). Lex. Poet adds the following meanings: *potestatem habere* (to have power), *possidere* (to hold), *valere* (to be strong) and deVries *raten* (to advise), *herschen* (to rule, to control), *erraten* (to work out).

Possible compassion or love driven advising is clearly out of the scope of *ráða* which is, in its present use, to be expected since this verb applies here to the runes. We can only hope that a sorcerer will aptly control his/her use of runic magic.

A famous example of lack of control in rune carving is found in Egill's saga (Ch. 73) where Egill cures a sick maid who undergone the effect of badly carved runes. Egill utters then a poem starting with:

Skalat maðr rúnar rísta,	Should-not a man runes <u>carve</u>
nema ráða vel kunni,	unless (he) to <u>control</u> well knows, (if he does no know well how to control them),
þat verðr mörgum manni,	it happens to many people
es of myrkvan staf villisk;	that by obscure stave-lore they miss the way.

2.3.3. *fáa* means 'to fetch, win, endure, give' and 'to draw, paint' (CV).

This verb has two different meanings and the one of 'to paint' seems to be meant in this stanza. Using blood as a 'paint' is attested in 'Grettir the Strong' saga (Ch. 79) where the witch in charge to kill Grettir selects a stump and

Síðan tók hún hníf sinn	then she took her knife
og <u>reist</u> rúnir á rótinni	and <u>carved</u> runes on the roots
og rauð í blóði sínu	and reddened (them) in <u>blood</u> hers
og kvað yfir <u>galdra</u>	and said upon a *galdr*.

The witch thus carves runes on the roots of the stump, and paints them with her own red blood.

2.3.4. *freista* means 'to try, tempt' (CV), deVries *versuchen* (to try).

Runes are now looked upon as being a trial or an opponent that checks your value and whose value you need to check. This kind of competitive relation evokes also the stress inherent to rune carving.

2.3.5. *biðja* means 'to beg' (CV and deVries).

LexPoet gives '*petere* (to seek, reach, obtain), *rogare* (to question)'. After the conversion, it took the meaning of 'to pray God'.

It is thus obvious that the meaning 'to beg' is the primary meaning of *biðja*. Its poetic use, however, suggest a much more active behavior than 'to beg'. To seek, to reach describe non passive ways to obtain something without waiting for a god (or, here a rune) that will fulfill our needs.

In § II-2.4 (stanza 145) we will learn of a relation between *biðja* and *blóta*: it seems that *blóta* (performing a blót) implies a request done to the god whom the blót is dedicated.

| *Betra er óbeðit* | Better he does not beg for |
| *in sé ofblótit,* | than over-sacrifices to the gods, |

Óðinn clearly is reluctant to fulfill to many such requests and associates them to over-sacrificial behavior.

2.3.6. *blóta* means 'to worship, sacrifice, curse' (CV) and deVries. *Opfern* (to sacrifice), *verheren* (to honor), *verfluchen* (to curse).

A first reaction can be to say that *blóta* has two main meanings that contradict each other: to worship and to curse. Our civilization visibly has put apart the two process to worship and to curse. That they may be confused in the ON language suggests two interpretations.

The first is that, since to worship is a religious attitude, this implies that to curse is also a religious attitude: ON religions seem to have casually accepted revenge and cursing, in what they do look being more savage and 'primitive' than our modern monotheisms that are supposed to at most to accept a moderate cursing. Not speaking of the past behaviors of these monotheisms, this last point can be argued against in view of the present behavior of several particular religious groups.

The second is that they have to be clearly recognized as depending on the context in which these verbs are used. What is religious, though, tends to be left implicit and only the reason of cursing is well explained. We can thus understand that, for instance, Sigurðr's revenge upon his father's killer must be seen as a complex religious 'curse' ceremony as described above in § I-8. We have to understand that the killing of his father has been itself the 'cursing' of a son who then can obliterate this curse by submitting the killer to a religious sacrifice, a kind of 'counter cursing' ceremony, known as 'bloody eagle'.

2.3.7. *senda* means 'to send, dedicate' (CV), deVries gives. *Senden* (to send), *töten* (to kill), and LexPoet *mittere* (to send, throw, dismiss). A ghost called by a wizard and sent against an enemy is called a *sending* (a sending) or rather, more properly, it consists in a string of embedded curses.

Sköp consist in a curse which is sent directly by a wizard to a cursed one. 'Sendings' are even worse since a dead soul will be in charge of acting the curse with no time limitation.

2.3.8. *sóa* means, for CV the same as *blóta* to sacrifice, and DeVries also gives. *Opfern* (to sacrifice), LexPoet provides three different meanings: 1. *serere* (to intertwine) 2. *consumere* (to spend, exhaust), *interficere* (to wipe out). If this is relative to a sacrifice, then *sóa* is much harsher than *blóta*. In stanza 109, the meaning 'to destroy' has been used to translate *sóit* (preterit of *sóa*).

In § 2.4 (stanza 145) we will learn of a relation between *senda* and *sóa*

ey sér til gildis gjöf;	ever (might) you be (*or* to you) to the proper value the gift;
betra er ósent	better he does not 'sends'

The first line says that a wizard should carefully balance the content of a curse with the amount of prejudice motivating this curse. The second line helps us to understand the full meaning of *sóa*: a sending must be handled with care because it amounts to wiping out who receives such a deadly gift, as LexPoet tells us.

We will come back to these points in next § 2.4, when dealing with Stanza 145.

II-2.4. *Do not step in another being's destiny: Hávamál 126 and 145*

stanza 126 Here are two possible translations of this stanza.

Commonplace understanding	**Magic understanding**
Would not be a shoe craftsman	Do not wield your art to move things
nor a shaft craftsman,	nor to stop an action (*or:* send a curse, as in s. 145),
unless you do them for yourself,	except when you deal with your own destiny,
if a shoe is ill-shaped	if things do not move anymore
or a shaft is bent	or if your action (*or* sending) turns badly,
then misfortune will be called on you.	then hatred will fall down upon you.

The commonplace interpretation gives two precise examples of social activity and social penalties associated to failures to fulfill a role. It is clear that we could say the same of any kind of trade. The fury recently fallen on medical doctors, while they have been protected until then by their high specialization, gives us a current example of it. All this is however absurd: What the craft of a craftsman is good to if he/she should work for him/herself only?

The two examples given in this stanza are very significant if they are understood as metaphors. The metaphor associated with shoes is probably associated to the situation in which the wizard is supposed to solve a problem, and the one associated to arrows is the one in which the wizard has to stop or to send a curse. Thus, Óðinn's advice is understood as: "Do not block the course of other people's örlög, let them solve this kind of problems by themselves."

Note that cursing wizards spend their time intruding in other people's örlög whereas healing wizards try to help their customers to find back a way to örlög's normal course, including a backing to accept death, and essentially aim at helping their customers to stop their self-damage.

In all cases, Óðinn's advice amounts to: "Don't be so eager for power, and never use it without weighing its dangers."

Stanza 145

Text	Literal translation in pseudo-English
Betra er óbeðit	Better he does not ask for
in sé ofblótit,	than over-sacrifices to the gods,
ey sér til gildis gjöf;	ever (might) you be (*or* to you)
	to the proper value the gift
betra er ósent	Better he does not dispatch (and even kills)
en sé ofsóit.	than too much use (possibly up to 'wiping out').
Svá Þundr of reist	Thus Þundr (Óðinn) carved
fyr þjóða rök,	[*fyr rök = rök* ahead] **future destiny** of the people
þar hann upp of reis,	there he up rose
er hann aftr of kom.	who him again came.

Translation

Better to avoid asking
than 'over-sacrificing' to the gods,

always (might) the gift for you be at the proper value,
Better to avoid dispatching
than over use (magic).
Thus Þundr (Óðinn) carved
the people's future örlög
there he rose up (after catching the runes)
him who came back
[from hanging on Yggdrasill].

Comment on the vocabulary

The translation of "***fyr*** *þjóða* ***rök*** …" by "the future örlög of the people …" will be explained when we will have met other examples using the word *rök*, in § II-3, 4, 5 and 7.

As a reminder to § II-2.3. above, remember that sacrifice (*blót*) must not exceed a given measure, and that *sóa* is much stronger than *blóta*.

Comment on the meaning of the stanza

This stanza clearly announces that *biðja* and *senda* are magic activities that must be very seldom or never practiced, and that *blóta* and *sóa* should never be applied in excess.

It is not really necessary to ask/beg (*biðja*) something from magic or from the gods, nor to dispatch (*senda*) spells or curses, unless your goal is to kill someone. A comparison with their Christian equivalent will help to understand the meaning of these two verbs: see how much Christians are keen to ask something (it is often the base of a 'prayer' to their God) and hate the idea of dispatching someone (this is criminal 'black' magic). In other words, Óðinn says, without including here any particular ethical judgment, that both requests and curses are possible but not primarily important.

It is dangerous to overdo sacrifices to the gods (*blóta*) and 'wiping out' someone (*sóa*). Here again, no ethical judgment but a similar opposition to Christian habits, though we need to replace the idea of sacrifice by the one of an offering, more Christian than a pagan sacrifice. Óðinn says that we should not exaggerate the practice of sacrifices (*or* offerings) while the Christians are fond of offerings to their God. Óðinn says that one should not exaggerate the practice of harming magic in order to murder one's enemies, while Christians loathe the idea of magic murder. We also see that these lines enable us to specify the meaning given here to the verbs *senda* and *sóa*. The first means probably 'to send a spell' without any specific will to kill, while the second certainly means 'to wipe out an opponent by killing him/her'.

We should add a few words on the ethics associated to Óðinn's advice. Fighting criminals usually relies on two opposed principles. The one tries to eliminate criminals, the other thinks better to 'manage' criminality so as decreasing its social impact. Hating criminals has been since long proven to be ineffective while criminality management is still under discussion and testing. In this stanza, Óðinn clearly takes sides for a 'controlled magic criminality'. More generally, Óðinn's advice in whole Hávamál shows zero compassion (and 'empathy' is reserved to and recommended to Norse contractual friendship—Hávamál s. 44: "*geði skaltu við þann blanda*" you must '*blend*' in spirit with him) though it goes with ethics favoring an as harmonious as possible society, "things being what they are."

II-2.5. On Sköp: *Stanzas 84 and 98*

These stanzas describe *sköp*, a less constraining version of fate than örlög.

This is a convenient place to recall that a commented translation is available as given in the bibliography, in which is given a thorough answer to the question: "Does Hávamál say that women are frivolous?" Readers may use this translation to look further into this aspect. The question we are asking now is: Does this stanza implicitly call upon the concept of destiny?

Stanza 84

ON	Literal translation	English translation
Meyjar orðum	Of a maid the words	In the words of a girl
skyli manngi trúa	should no man have confidence	no man should have confidence
né því, er kveðr kona,	nor what, is to say [*or* sing, recite] a woman [*or* wife],	nor in what an (adult) woman says;
því at á hverfanda hvéli	because on a turning wheel	because on a revolving wheel

váru þeim hjörtu	were to them hearts	their hearts have been
sköpuð,	**shaped** [*or* created]	**shaped**,
brigð í brjóst of lagið.	breach in the (their) breast is lying.	cutting (*or* flexibility, *or* change *or* inconstancy) is lying in their chest.

In this stanza, the 'lack of confidence' is not due to their fickleness but to their breaching abality. Remember that the word used in line 5, *sköpuð*, is the past participle of verb *skapa* which means 'shaped' with all kinds of shapings, including the magic ones. We could also translate lines 5 by "their hearts are destined to" without changing the meaning nor evoking magic. We find another example of *sköpuð* in Reginsmál s. 6 (see § II-11), where the use of magic is obvious since it describes a curse sent by Loki on a person whose '*sköpuð*' will be damaging.

We thus should not forget that verb *skapa* past participle carries also the meaning of destiny shaping. Instead of translating line 5 by "women's heart is made/shaped/on a turning wheel" we can also understand it as "the curse of women's hearts is shaped on a turning wheel."

This is why it is wrong to understand these lines as a kind of jest *à la* Offenbach. Óðinn states women's fates, their *sköp* in this line 5. If he intends to imply that women are really 'fickle' … then for one he says a stupid thing, and for two, and more convincingly, the description of two women, provided in the following stanzas, does not fit at all this feature. *Billings mær* is incredibly crafty and cutting since she joins insult to rupture (see Hávamál s. 96–102). *Gunnlöð* is not at all frivolous nor cutting, she is the one broken by Óðinn, showing her weakness.

These two examples occur in worlds where women are not respected (remember that *Gunnlöð* is a Giantess), they have the choice between being cutting ('breaking') or being broken, which illustrates their *sköp*. Refusing the insult 'fickle' as a valid translation and accepting the meaning 'breaking' changes stanza 97 from being a bad joke into a social assessment of how girls have been taught and are often still taught nowadays. This understanding is nearer to a feminist complaint than a low rate joke.

Note also that, implicitly by stating their *sköp*, Óðinn suggests that this is not their örlög. In his worldview, women's *sköp* is shaped by other people, while their specific örlög is shaped by the Norns and is still largely unknown, as it is for anyone else.

Billings mær says:

Stanza 98

"Auk nær aftni	"Also near the evening
skaltu, Óðinn, koma,	you shall, Óðinn, come
ef þú vilt þér mæla man;	if you will request a mistress for you;
allt eru **ósköp**	all (we both) are **no-fate** (dead or cursed)
nema einir viti	except if (us) alone are aware
slíkan löst saman."	of our misbehavior."

The word *sköp* is prefixed here by the negation '*ó*' and we can understand it either as 'no-destiny', or as 'death'. In the sagas, it sometimes takes the meaning of 'curse'.

Billing's mær fakes being as eager as Óðinn for having sex together. She speaks of this behavior as a 'flaw' or, at least as 'misbehavior'. We may suppose that her aim is to definitively convince Óðinn to leave her quiet for now, promising to give him more pleasure next night. Her trick will fully succeed. We may ask why she thinks it necessary to resort to such a trick. There is nevertheless no need see another reason than Óðinn has been so insistent that she fears to be raped if she tersely refuses. We can see in s. 102 that Óðinn seems to have, afterwards, well understood that his greed pushed Billing's mær to mislead him as she did.

She is certainly a crafty one. 'Cheater' is even a little strong as long as she is trying to keep her freedom of having no unwanted sex. She is certainly nor 'unfaithful' nor 'fickle'. This still substantiates our interpretation for *brigð* ('cutting, sharp' rather than 'fickle') as in stanza 84.

In conclusion, *sköp* could be seen from a modern atheist's view either as thought over personal choices or as social constraints imposed by some lobbies that think these constraints are justified. Since magic pervades Ancient Scandinavia, these personal choices are often seen as produced by magic.

II-2.6. To be creative and knowledgeable: Stanza 141

I then became fertile
and was full of knowledge
and grew and well throve,

a word, out of my speech,
looked for another word,
a deed, out of my deeds,
looked for another deed.

Stanza 141 explains how Óðinn obtained a harmonious destiny, according to which his spirit is fertile and his life is prosperous. The 'recipe' is given by the four last lines: if your deeds and words intermingle in a harmonious evolution, without ever hampering each other, you then deserve a harmonious destiny, as the one described in the first three lines. The way in which these two capacities operate and are laid out determines chaotic destinies—known as unhappy ones– and the harmonious ones—known as happy.

Let us nevertheless observe that the advice provided here is not easy to follow. Admittedly past words and action always interact with the future ones, but a great sincerity associated to a very clear mind are necessary so that the actions and the words of past do not hamper those of the future if they interact as Óðinn recommends it.

While avoiding speaking about destiny, we would say that a harmonious life proceeds when none of the dreams of youth are disavowed in the ripe or old age, which underlines in another way how seldom this happens.

Absence of later disavowal of one's past values could well be the modern definition of 'fate' which is the nearest to what has been Old Norse örlög.

II–2.7. Rational Conscious Thinking and Magic: how a wizard should think: Stanzas 18, 26, 27, 28, 63, 141

It happens several times that Óðinn describes how a character (say, n° 1) may have to deal with problems associated to his/her lack of wisdom (e.g. in s. 26 and 27), or associated to wisdom acquisition (s. 63) where the needed knowledge is relative to another character n° 2. The forthcoming examples show clearly that Óðinn does not confuse at all these situations with those that require introspective knowledge relative to character n° 1 him/herself.

Section 2.7.1 will describe the first situation that will enable us, in § 2.7.2 to observe how differently Óðinn conveys situations that include some amount of self-thinking.

§ II-2.7.1. *Magic sent towards other people than the sorcerer*

s. 26

Literal translation	Pseudo-English translation:	English translation:
Ósnotr maðr	A non-wise human	An unwise person
þykkisk allt vita,	thinks himself all to know,	thinks himself as all-knowing,
ef hann á sér í vá veru;	if he to self in a wretched shelter;	if he owns a wretched shelter.
hittki hann veit,	non-hits [does not understand] he knows,	He does not know to hit (on the idea of)
hvat hann skal við kveða,	what he shall 'with' say,	what to say to others
ef hans freista firar.	If him to try [*or* to tempt] people [*nom. plur. = subject of* freista].	if people try him.

The first three lines describe an individual n°1 who is stupidly proud of his/her (cheap) knowledge. The three last ones say that he/she is unable to comprehend what other people (n°2 etc.) are going to think of him/her.

Stanza 27 describes how other people react to a character's dumbness if he/she "speaks too much."

s. 27

Ósnotr maðr	A non-wise human
er með aldir kemr,	who with others comes
þat er bazt, at hann þegi;	that is best, for him to stay silent;
engi þat veit,	none who knows
at hann ekki kann,	at him non can [that he can nothing]
nema hann mæli til margt;	except he (that he) speaks very much;
veit-a maðr	knows-not a human
hinn er vettki veit,	he who nothing knows
þótt hann mæli til margt.	in spite of that he speaks very much.

Next stanza describes how a candidate to wisdom should interact with acknowledged wise ones in order to be accepted among them. The last three lines explain that the candidate should also avoid sharing too much his/her knowledge outside of the circle that he/she wishes to integrate.

s. 63

Fregna ok segja	Ask and say
skal fróðra hverr,	shall of the wise ones who,
sá er vill heitinn horskr,	he who will be named wise,
einn vita	one to know
né annarr skal,	not another shall,
þjóð veit, ef þrír ro [=eru].	the people know, if three are.

The three above examples show the kind of vocabulary Óðinn uses when he describes the classical relationship among several characters: the one where a character n°1 wishes to interact with another person n°2 etc.

We shall now see four examples where Óðinn's speech completely deviates from this configuration: here character n°1 wishes to interact with him/herself, what is currently called 'introspection'.

§ II-2.7.2. Self-applied magic

s. 18

Sá einn veit	Who the one is mindful [*or* aware, conscious]
er víða ratar	who far travels
ok hefr fjölð of farit,	and raises [*or:* starts] much of 'for travelling'
hverju geði	what state of mind
stýrir gumna hverr,	leads the men such that [leads such men]
sá er vitandi er vits.	**who is 'being mindful' is [*or:* he who]** **'of *or* towards mindfulness'.**

The way of speech in the last line of s. 18 may be understood as being aware of another one's thought, as any clever person should. We must however take into account what Óðinn states in famous s. 138, that he was "given to Óðinn, *sjalfur sjalfum mér* 'me to myself'," where he claims interacting with himself. There is thus a second possible understanding to s. 18, namely that Óðinn speaks of someone who is aware of his/her own awareness. This is of a completely different nature as singled out by Carl G. Jung ("The Structure and Dynamics of the Psyche," 2nd edition, Routledge 2014, pp. 187–189):

"Between 'I do this' and 'I am conscious of doing this' [*almost verbatim Óðinn's "being mindful of mindfulness" except that Óðinn addresses an 'I am conscious of being conscious'*] there is a world of difference, amounting sometimes to outright contradiction. Consequently, there is a consciousness in which unconsciousness predominate, as well as a conscious in which self-consciousness predominates (*this is Óðinn's version*) … So, we come to the paradoxical conclusion that there is no conscious content which is not in some other respect unconscious."

Jung's last sentence is cited here in order to show what is, in his own worldview, the important outcome of "I am conscious of doing this." It carries a possibility of interaction between our conscious and our unconscious—a central theme of Jung's philosophy. Óðinn's position goes less far: he 'simply' marvels at the existence of introspection in humankind's way of thinking.

We may also call to stanzas 28 and 141 that express a 'consciousness of being conscious' as s. 18 and 138 do.

s. 28

Fróðr sá þykkisk,	Learned so self-thinks
er fregna kann	who ask questions can
ok segja it sama,	and speak it together;
eyvitu leyna	nothing [*or* lack of wit] hide
megu ýta synir,	they can of men the sons
því er gengr um guma.	because that it goes among humans.

This stanza immediately follows s. 27 conclusion that a wise one should avoid blabbering about one's own knowledge. In its first line, the reflexive form of *þykkisk = þykkja—self* (to think of oneself) which may, as in English, simply carry a hint to self-delusion. Note that s. 28 does not seem to hint at irony, which supports an interpretation nearer to an introspective attitude.

Stanza 141 is now totally unambiguous when it describes an active way of thinking–as opposed to a somewhat passive introspection:

s. 141

Þá nam ek frævask	Then became I fertile
ok fróðr vera	and full of knowledge was

ok vaxa ok vel hafask,	and grew and well throve,
orð mér af orði	a word out of my word
orðs leitaði,	a word looked for help
verk mér af verki	a deed out of my deed
verks leitaði.	a deed looked for help.

Be it shaped from words or deeds, a fertile knowledge is here evolving under an interaction with oneself, as does the 'mindful traveler' of stanza 18.

II-3. VafÞrúðnismál and Grímnismál

VafÞrúðnismál twice contains the form *skópu* (s. 25, 39) and three times *sköpuð* (s. 21, 29, 35).

Grímnismál twice contains the form *sköpuð* (s. 40, 41).

These are two mythological poems that explain, among other things, how our Earth (*Jörð*) was formed, shaped by the gods using various body parts of the primary giant, Ymir. VafÞrúðnismál stanza 21 and Grímnismál 40 are almost identical:

VafÞrúðnismál 21	**Literal Translation**
1. *Ór Ymis holdi*	From Ymir's flesh
2. *var jörð of* **sköpuð**,	has been earth **shaped**,
3. *en ór beinum björg,*	though from his bones, cliffs,
4. *himinn ór hausi*	sky from his skull
5. *ins hrímkalda jötuns,*	of him frost-cold giant,
6. *en ór sveita sær.*	though from his sweat, the sea.

Grímnismál 40

Ór Ymis holdi (1 Vaf.)

var jörð of **sköpuð**, (2 Vaf.)

en ór sveita sær, (6 Vaf.)

björg ór beinum, (3 Vaf.)

baðmr ór hári, (literally: 'tree, from his hair')

en ór hausi himinn. (4 Vaf.)

VafÞrúðnismál 29, 35 and Grímnismál 41 again use the past participle *sköpuð* for saying that the ground or the clouds have been worked out by the gods. In all these cases, even if we refuse to consider the concept of 'earth destiny', earth shaping by the gods is an operation held with some magic. To say that the gods have 'manufactured or done' Earth amounts to hiding this magic aspect. Besides, using the verb 'to create' on the one hand belongs to the vocabulary of Christian myths and on the other hand it is inaccurate here since this 'creation' started with Ymir's dismemberment. It would be then more exact to say than they have 'shaped Earth's fate' which renders the presence of magic when using the past participle *sköpuð*.

VafÞrúðnismál 42 provides a further example of the use of the word *rök*:

Óðinn kvað:	*Óðinn said:*
"Seg þú þat it tólfta,	"Say in twelfth
*hví þú **tíva rök***	you who the **god's rök** (örlög)
***öll**, Vafþrúðnir, vitir"*	**entirety**, Vafþrúðnir, is informed"
	(you, Vafþrúðnir, who knows all the gods' rök)

This could allude either to magic knowledge ("you know the origin and the causes of the gods") or a factual knowledge ("you fully know the gods' related mythology"). This being said, it is not certain that Ancient Norse people would have seen a difference between these two formulations.

This is why it seems more reasonable to think, as that will become clear in Alvíssmál § 5, that "gods' rök" points at this part of the universal örlög specifically describing the gods' örlög.

II-4. Lokasenna

Stanza 21

Óðinn kvað:	*Óðinn said:*
Ærr ertu, Loki,	Mad are you, Loki
ok örviti,	and not-clever
er þú fær þér Gefjun at gremi,	that you bring to you Gefjon in wrath
*því at aldar **örlög***	because humankind's **örlög**,
hygg ek, at hon öll of viti	think I, to her all knowledgeable,
jafngörla sem ek.	equally-clearly as I (do).

Aldar is the genitive of *öld* = a large duration of time, an age. In poetry this word takes the meaning of humankind/people/all existing beings.

This stanza adds credit to the belief that Gefjon, Frigg and Óðinn knew everyone's örlög, that encompasses past and future.

Stanza 25

Frigg kvað:	Frigg said:
Örlögum ykkrum	Of **örlög** to you both
skylið aldregi	you should never
segja seggjum frá,	tell humankind among (among humankind)
hvat it æsir tveir	what you, Æsir twofold,
drýgðuð í árdaga;	you committed at times ancient;
firrisk æ **forn rök** firar.	Let (them) avoid forever **old 'deeds'** (past örlög), human ones.

Loki has criticized just before, in s. 24, some of Óðinn's behavior and Frigg recommends to Loki avoiding to speak of Óðinn's örlög or of his own. This is the first time he gets the advice to be silent about past events. Boyer skillfully translates: "What belongs to the past has to remain in the past" and this translation well renders the idea that the gods seek to hide something to human beings.

The expression used by Frigg to speak of these 'old deeds' is *forn rök*. The popular meaning of the English word 'destiny' (which refers to future events) does not agree at all to the context. In a translation it will thus be necessary to choose a translation as 'old deeds', i.e. historical facts while "old örlög" indicates the örlög of past times, still existing as written in runes by the Norns, thus still fully active. In this instance, *rök* is used in order to indicate a special part of the whole örlög, here the past.

Thus, Frigg affirms that there are old stories about which it is better not to speak. The need for hiding "what everyone knows but that nobody says" is clearly rejected by Loki who goes on revealing gods' past without restraint. Moreover, Loki's answer to Frigg strikes back at once: in stanza 28 he states "I am the reason why you cannot see any more Baldr riding in the halls," which stresses that he has been responsible twice for Baldr's death: once by inducing Höðr to kill him, twice by refusing to cry at his death.

Stanza 29

Freyja kvað:	*Freyja said:*
Ærr ertu, Loki,	Mad are you, Loki
er þú <u>yðra</u> telr	that you to <u>both</u> say
ljóta <u>leiðstafi</u>;	ugly <u>hateful-'runes'</u>;
örlög *Frigg*	**örlög** Frigg
hygg ek at öll viti,	think I in all is known
þótt hon sjálfgi segi.	though she not-herself speaks (of it).

As in stanza 25, line 2 alludes to the dialogue of two persons by using the dative case of 'thou' in the plural = 'to you' (*yðra*).

Loki has insulted Frigg in s. 28 and Freyja again tells him, as Frigg did in s. 25, that some things must remain unspoken of. It is obvious that Loki is the one who insists in revealing unpleasant truths to the gods and he obstinately refuses to stay silent.

Lines 3 uses the form *leiðr-stafr* = hateful-*stafr*. The word *stafr* means a staff and it is also used to designate a staff carved with runes, i.e. a runic inscription. Since Norns carve örlög in runes, it is not surprising that 'staff' might be directly understood as 'runes' and to speak of "hateful runes." Boyer translates by "hateful charms", Dronke by "hatefulnesses" and Orchard by "horrible deeds." This illustrates the tendency of the American school to systematically refuse to evoke magic in their interpretations, as long as it does not produce nonsense.

It should also be noted that Freyja's words: "*hon sjálfgi segi* (she herself does not speak)" could be interpreted as Frigg being unable to speak about örlög. The last line of s. 25 indicates that she avoids speaking of it because it is better for humankind to "*firrisk æ* (avoid always)" this knowledge, especially when related to the past. Hávamál stanza 56 (§ II-2.1) hints at the same idea.

From all these debates, comes out that the concept of 'past örlög' is obvious for the Æsir, which is not rendered by the commonplace meaning of 'destiny'. When Gefjon, Óðinn and Frigg are said to know all of örlög, this implies that they know the past as well as the future. In other words, Germanic örlög are not associated to a multiple temporality: they are as one temporal block, fully present at each moment. This consolidates the refusal to see in each of the three Norns the now classical image relating them to segments of time, we call past, present and future (see Völuspá stanza 20 comments § II-1.4).

This stanza 20 also says that Norns write örlög, and "Writings remain," i.e. what has been written will exist out of time. But "speech flies away" and this why, in addition to the arguments presented in stanza 20, its last lines cannot use "*segja*" which implies they state the örlög: Stated only örlög fly away at the first blow of time whereas, when they are carved, they become timeless.

Note that sköp may be destroyed by erasing their runes while örlög timelessness is guaranteed by the Norns' inaccessibility.

Stanza 27

Frigg kvað:	Frigg said:
Veiztu, ef ek inni ættak	Know-you, if here I had
Ægis höllum i	Ægir's hall into
Baldri líkan bur,	Baldr similar son,
út þú né kvæmir	outside you could not come
frá ása sonum,	from the Æsir sons
ok væri þá at þér vreiðum vegit.	and he would to you angrily carried/have fought/have killed.

This stanza does not specifically speak of destiny but it underlines how much Frigg's sköp failed to modify Baldr's örlög.

Frigg's fury, expressed here in such a fierce way, undoubtedly reveals her frustration and guilt feelings. She feels guilty because she revealed that Baldr was protected from all natural forces, except mistletoe. She is frustrated because all her magic failed to protect her son. This is also an example of örlög powers: if the Norns took care of including any event in someone's örlög, no amount of magic, here called *sköp*, is able to prevent from it.

Frigg used all her knowledge of magic to protect her son, i.e. she formulated the most powerful possible sköp in order to protect him and she could note their impotence when opposed to örlög, whereas a more subtle use of skillful sköp could undoubtedly have prolonged Baldr's lifespan for some length of time (and even for a potentially infinite one). We begin to understand why sköp may modify someone's destiny, though only in the case where they do not oppose to his/her örlög.

You will find in chapter IV of the present book more details on the possible unconscious links among the triplet 'Frigg, Baldr, mistletoe' as it is explained by Carl Jung (1967) pp. 258–9, § 392–393.

II-5. Alvíssmál

s. 9

Segðu mér þat Alvíss,	Tell me Alvíss,
*—**öll** of **rök** fira*	**all** of **örlög** [past and future] of <u>humankind</u>
vörumk, dvergr, at vitir	foresee, dwarf, you get the meanings …

This poem tells how Þórr checked a dwarf's mythological knowledge. He used thirteen times a fixed formula, translated below, before stating his questions. In this case, we could obviously translate *rök* by destiny but, as in VafÞrúðnismál and Grímnismál, the meaning 'events' or 'story' are also possible. Owing to the fact that, in Lokasenna, we noted that *rök* is used to indicate a facet of örlög, and that the stanza below deals with the *rök* of humankind, it seems justified to see in "***rök** fira*", just above, humankind's örlög, as in Lokasenna (§ II-4), s. 25 "ancient rök" points at "ancient örlög." This meaning of *rök* (specific facets of örlög), seems to be valid in poetic Edda, it will become its accepted meaning in the conclusion of this chapter.

II-6. Helgakviða hundingsbana hin fyrri

This ballad of Helgi, Hunding's killer, speaks of an antique hero, a king whose life, since his birth, has been driven by the Norns. The first stanzas of the *kviða* tell of their influence on Helgi at his birth. In s. 2 the Norns are behaving as fairies are told to behave in several middle age tales.

s. 2

Nótt varð í bæ,	Night was in place,
nornir kómu,	the Norns came,
þær er öðlingi	they to the king,
<u>*aldr of skópu;*</u>	<u>life-time shaped.</u>
þann báðu fylki frægstan verða	they begged lands (and) most famous be
ok buðlunga	and a king
beztan þykkja.	best self-willed.

The Norns 'beg' lands for the king. The meaning of verb *biðja* (here as *báðu*) is explained in § II-2.3, above.

Skópu is preterit plural of verb *skapa*. That it expresses a magic shaping is obvious in the present context.

Noun *aldr* means an age and carries the idea of 'old' as shown by its several meanings: life-period, old age, a long period of time and 'eternity'.

Next stanza explains how this <u>life-time</u>, after having been <u>shaped</u>, was secured by the Norns.

s. 3

Sneru þær af afli <u>örlögþáttuþá</u>	Twisted they successfully (his) <u>örlög story-line</u>
er borgir braut	then walls broke
í Bráluni;	in Brálund;
þær of greiddu	they disentangled, interpreted
gullin <u>símu</u>	the <u>ropes</u> of gold
ok und mánasal miðjan festu.	and under moon's hall in the middle fastened them.

Sneru (or *snöru*) is the preterit plural of verb *snúa*, to twist.

A *þáttr* properly means a single strand of a rope but took also the meaning of a 'short story' and an Islandic long story is a 'saga' while a short one is a 'þáttr'.

In the first line, 'they' points at the Norns since *þær* is the plural of 'she', and '(his)' at the baby Helgi still is. The Norn's actions seem to destroy the castle in which this ceremony takes place, and it proceeds under the sky (the 'moon hall').

The 'ropes of gold' are 'Helgi's strands of his story-line' and that the Norns have to disentangle them in order to interpret them. This job is quite energy consuming and this fits with the fact that they are supposed to be written in runes.

This may seem strange because they need a lot of work to understand their own runes, and we may suppose that this stanza expresses that they wrote them in a state of trance that means interpretation, as well known for many other foreseers.

II-7. Völundarkviða

The comments given here refer to Völundarkviða various episodes.
If you do not remember the details of this poem, it would be handy to have
a look at the illustrated version of the 'tale of Völundr'.

Stanza 1

Meyjar flugu sunnan,	The maidens fled (from) South,
myrkvið í gögnum,	dark-wood through,
alvitr unga,	full of wisdom (was) a young one,
örlög <u>*drýgja;*</u>	**örlög** <u>to endure/carry out/commit.</u>

Verb *drýgja* is very polysemic. CV gives "to commit, perpetrate, especially in a pejorative meaning, for example, *drýgja hórdóm* = 'to commit'
prostitution." The translators have, in the case of *örlög drýgja*, selected: "to
try one's luck." DeVries does not give this meaning but the ones of 'to
carry out/endure' which are thus closer to the etymological meaning of
this verb. LexPoet gives the basic meaning of *facere* = to achieve, and adds
a great number of examples showing that, in Norse, it can take many possible meanings, going from 'to indulge' or 'to endure' until 'to perpetrate'.
It thus seems that CV's "especially pejorative" meaning is not as obvious as
he states, at least in poetry.

Stanza 3

sjö vetr at þat	Seven winters at that (they remained)
en inn átta	but the eighth one
allan þráðu	all they longed
en inn níunda	but the ninth
nauðr um skildi;	**need split** (them);
meyjar fýstusk	the maidens wished (to go)
á myrkvan við,	towards dark-wood,
alvitr unga,	full of wisdom (was) a young one,
örlög *drýgja.*	**örlög** to endure/carry out/commit.

The feminine substantives *nauð* and *nauðr* mean 'need'. It is the name of rune Naudiz (Nauð in Norse). In our description of each Norn's role (see above Völuspá stanza 20 §II-1.4), it would be thus Norn Skuld who is implied in the maidens' departure. We understand that a person indifferent to runes will find this remark stretchy. On another hand, we cannot imagine how a rune magic knowledgeable Norse person could be unaware of this hint.

The use of the verb *drýgja* when evoking the achievement of a destiny deserves the following precise comments.

* * * (drýgja)

First of all, remember that Frigg already used *drýgja* in Lokasenna s. 25. She says to Loki: "*hvat it to æsir to tveir drýgðuð í árdaga*, (what you, the double god, <u>perpetrated</u> in the olden days)" as being part of his örlög.

Other typical instances of using verb *drýgja* in poetic Edda are as follows.

Atlamál in grænlenzku

s. 45 "*Hvat úti drýgðu* (what outside 'happened')" is the massacre of a guest, therefore to translate *drýgðu* by '<u>was perpetrated</u>' is valid.

s. 86 Guðrún announces to Atli that she has killed their children. He answers by warning her that he will kill her and adds: "*drýgt þú fyrr to hafðir* … (you <u>perpetrated</u> before …)".

Grímnismál

s. 35 "*Askr Yggdrasils drýgir erfiði* … Ash Yggdrasill <u>endures</u> a suffering."

Hárbarðsljóð

s. 48 Hárbarðr says to Þórr that his wife maintains a lover at his place and that when he returns "*þann muntu þrek drýgja*, (then you will have courage to practice)." In this context, 'courage practice' implies suffering and/or violence.

* * *

We see that the meanings of *drýgja* in Edda is the one of an action that is carried out either with violence or in enduring some suffering.

Völundarkviða thus teaches us that örlög cannot be carried out quietly: they are carried out with violence or they are received in suffering.

In the poem, the örlög of the *drýgjendi* (perpetrating, etc.) girls illustrate this rule. They do not seem themselves to suffer from the circumstances but rather to bring suffering: When they leave their lovers, Völundr's two brothers are desperate (they will go on to searching them and disappear from the story) and Völundr himself stays open to the terrible destiny awaiting him.

Comment on the meaning of stanzas 1 and 3

From the point of view of örlög, the girls' behavior confirms what we already know: that örlög are binding us tightly. These girls besides themselves add the necessity to fully assume their örlög without balking. They are divine beings, "coming from the south," and they are certainly steered by their örlög although being foreigners. Moreover, the two quoted stanzas state that these ladies are 'full of wisdom'. To say that they are very wise means that they are also knowledgeable, in particular about magic. We now understand why they leave their lovers without balking because they are informed of their örlög and what exactly means assuming one's örlög.

> Here is an active use of örlög. Some beings can perpetrate them, some others endure them. It is not surprising that, according to circumstances, the poets insisted on a different facet of örlög. We can certainly see here a "web of contradictions", but we may also choose to see here the richness of this concept.

II-8. Grípisspá

The poem Völuspá ('Völva's-prophecy') clearly shows that a *völva* is able to prophesy (*spá*). We can also say that a *völva* is a *spákona* (prophecy-woman) or *spámær* (prophecy-maiden). These forms are also the ones used for men and Grípir is a *spámaðr* (prophecy-man), the masculine equivalent of a *völva*, and the name of the poem means 'Grípir's prophecy'.

A prose introduction tells that "*hann ... var allra manna vitrastr ok framvíss.* (He was ... of all men the wisest and the most certain (or wisest) about the future)." We must notice that Grípir is Sigurðr's maternal uncle. In Germanic tales in general, we know that the maternal uncle very often has major bonds with his nephew. He may even raise him as a foster father. Here, he will be in charge of teaching him his destiny (*örlög*), i.e. what kind of life örlög will coerce on him.

Sigurðr requires of him to state his future. Grípir is not very willing to tell Sigurðr's örlög and he begins to evoke the past, Sigurðr's father murder, (4 first lines of s. 9). He then tells to Sigurðr a part of his future: he will kill his father's murderers and that will free him from Reginn's sköp:

s. 9

Fyrst muntu fylkir	First will you, prince,
föður of hefna,	your father revenge,
ok Eylima	and from Eylimi
alls harms reka,	all crimes retaliate,
þú munt harða	you will, the hard
Hundings sonu	Hunding's sons,
snjalla fella,	boldly fall down;
muntu sigr hafa.	you will victory obtain.

s.11

Muntu einn vega	You alone will slay
orm inn frána,	the worm (serpent, dragon) gleaming,
þann er gráðugr liggr	which greedy lies
á Gnitaheiði,	on Gnítaheiðr;
þú munt báðum	you shall both
at bana verða	to death bring,
Regin ok Fáfni;	Regin and Fáfnir.
rétt segir Grípir.	truth tells Gripir.

He then tells of Sigurðr's meeting with Sigrdrífa, he describes her as being beautiful of look and raised by a king named Heimir. Sigurðr answers as follows:

Sigurðr kvað:	**Sigurðr said:**	**Translation:**
28.		
"Hvat er mik at því,	"What is it to me,	What matters to me

þótt mær séi	though the maiden might be	that the girl is
fögr áliti	fair of look	beautiful of aspect and
fædd at Heimis?	nurtured by Heimir?	risen by Heimir?
Þat skaltu Grípir	That you must Grípir	It is necessary that, Grípir,
görva segja,	clearly and enough tell	clearly and without restriction
því at þú öll of sér	since for you all foresee	you say all what you foresee
örlög fyrir."	**örlög** before (me)."	of my future **örlög**.

Then, Grípir tells that both Sigrdrífa and him will deeply love each other but

31.

It munuð alla	You will want all
eiða vinna	oaths work
fullfastliga,	fully-firm
fá munuð halda;	little will you hold;

Sigurðr is of course indignant at his own (future) fickleness, and Grípir must explain the causes of this fickleness and he cannot anymore hide something from him.

In Lokasenna, we have seen örlög indicating the past, in Völundarkviða timeless örlög manifested themselves at their own will. Here, at the beginning of the poem we meet the örlög of the past in the four first lines of s. 9 then the future in the last four lines and in s. 11, 28 and 31 (and until s. 53).

In the last stanza, we understand that Grípir is quite concerned to have told the whole truth to a fighter as dangerous as Sigurðr, famous for his angers. Not without some elegance, however, the last at once quiets down Grípir in the two first lines of stanza 53. He says:

| "Skiljum heilir, | "Let us separate happy, |
| **mun-at sköpum** vinna ..." | we **cannot on the sköp** win..." |

This conclusion is noticeable because Sigurðr does not cite örlög but sköp, seemingly confusing them. He obviously knows that örlög are nothing else than Norns kind of sköp. But Norse culture states that örlög decisions are impossible to circumvent, as opposed to sköp that can be modified by their creator. We understand here that Sigurðr uses 'Norn's sköp' as a way of speech (a *kenning*) for örlög: he knows that he has to sustain his örlög and he does not go further than using a kenning to hint at an impossible resistance to them.

II-9. Fáfnismál

(The poem starts with a prose introduction):

Sigurðr and Reginn leave to find Fáfnir and they spot the path he follows between his cave and the river where he waters himself. Reginn disappears hiding in a close moor while Sigurðr digs a pit that crosses Fáfnir's path. When Fáfnir appears, spitting his poison, Sigurðr is hardly touched by it. As Fáfnir passes above him, he pierces Fáfnir's heart with his sword. Fáfnir does not die at once, and they exchange some words with each other. Fáfnir says to him: "*it gjalla gull / ok it glóðrauða fé* (this howling gold and this wealth red as embers) will bring death to you."

(He adds)

Fáfnir kvað:	Literally	Translation
11.		
Norna dóm	Norns' doom	The doom of the Norns,
þú munt fyr nesjum hafa	you will in front of the nesses have	you will meet while sailing
ok örlög ósvinns apa	and an örlög of an unwise monkey	and an idiotic monkey's örlög
…	…	…
alt er feigs forað.	all is danger to the sentenced ones.	all is danger to a sentenced one.

In this stanza, Fáfnir attempts cursing Sigurðr but we know that he will not drown "in front of a ness" and will not become either an "idiotic monkey." Here, the sköp are ineffective because they are not grounded in some real knowledge that Fáfnir would have about Sigurðr. At least, it confirms that Norn's örlög will be catastrophic. The following stanza shows that Fáfnir holds a great deal of knowledge and that Sigurðr knows about that.

Sigurðr, as he did with Grípir, seeks to receive a teaching. Here is their deeply instructive exchange:

s. 12.	Literally	Translation
Segðu mér Fáfnir …	Tell me Fáfnir …	Tell me Fáfnir …
hverjar ro þær **nornir,**	which are these **Norns**,	which are these 'Norns',
er nauðgönglar ro	who go to those in need (*or* who are need-walkers)	who go to those of need (*or* who wander on the ways of need)
ok kjósa	and choose/part/ bewitch	and split (sometimes by sorcery)
mæðr frá mögum.	mothers from (their) sons.	mothers from their sons. (they grant a safe birth to women)

s. 13. *Fáfnir kvað:*		Translation
Sundrbornar mjök	Different-born much	They are born from various origins,
segi ek **nornir** *vera,*	I say **Norns** are,	the 'Norns ', I say,
eigu-t þær ætt saman,	have-not they family the same,	are not from one family,
sumar ro áskunngar,	some are of the Æsir family	some are of the Æsir family
sumar alfkunngar,	some of the elves,	some of the elves,
sumar dætr Dvalins.	some Dvalinn's daughters.	some are Dvalinn's daughters (Dvalinn is the dwarves' father)

At first, let us note that these two stanzas seem to confuse Norns and Dísir. Norns do not wander around, the three of them are of Giants birth and they do not deal with childbirth. Moreover, in stanza 11 Fáfnir correctly allots örlög management to them. In stanza 12, Sigurðr raises questions that point at Dísir but uses the word Norn. Either Fáfnir also confuses Norns and Dísir or he understands it as a *heiti*, made obvious by the just enounced contradictions. The use of *heiti* being so widespread in Norse poetry, it seems that the second assumption is most probable.

Other poems teach us that the divinities who govern childbirth are called *Dísir*, (in the singular, one *Dís*) instead of being called Norns.

Lastly, Fáfnir informs us about the origins of the Dísir (here '*heiti*-ed' as Norns) that seem to be quite varied as opposed to the Norn's. As long as the Dísir are closer to individual fates than of the one of the Universe, it is not surprising that each divine race provides its own 'leaders of the shapings' to humans.

In the following stanza (s. 14) Sigurðr uses a striking metaphor to speak of Ragnarök. He points at it by *er blanda hjörlegi/Surtr ok Æsir saman* (they merge the sword-lake/Surtr and the Æsir them together) [*legi* is the dative of *lögr*, a lake and the rune Laukaz. Sword-lake is blood]. During Ragnarök, the Giants, personified here by Surtr, and the Æsir will destroy *saman* (each other) and thus the blood of these two groups will merge. He uses this metaphor to ask Fáfnir where Ragnarök will take place and Fáfnir answers: "*Óskópnir hann heitir* (it is called 'Unshaped one')" and this may imply that the place where Ragnarök will take place is not yet 'worked out'. Hrafnagaldur stanzas 2 to 5 (see bibliography) provide a hint of the sköp that will shape this place so that Ragnarök might occur.

Finally, Fáfnir announces to Sigurðr that Reginn will betray and kill him, just as he has been betrayed. (s. 22):

"*Reginn mik réð,*   Reginn me advised and betrayed,
han þik ráða mun ...and you betray and advise he will ...."

When Fáfnir is dead, Reginn reappears and recalls that Sigurðr has recently killed his brother "though he is partially guilty himself," he thus threatens Sigurðr of some kind of revenge. The last replies in two points. First, he recalls that he would never have attempted to kill Fáfnir if Reginn had not pushed him over the edge by questioning his courage. Second, he also recalls that Reginn behaved like a coward: While he, Sigurðr, fought with the dragon, he, Reginn hid somewhere in a close moor (s. 28)

"*afli mínu*   strength mine
atta ek við orms megin, I [had to exert] against the dragon's power
meðan þú í lyngvi látt   while you in a moor were lying."

Then, Reginn goes to Fáfnir's corpse, extracts his heart and drinks the blood running from this wound. He feels tired after having drunk all this blood and he asks Sigurðr to cook Fáfnir's heart while he sleeps to recover.

While cooking the heart, Sigurðr checks if the heart is well-cooked, burns his hand and put a finger in his mouth. Then, at once: (literal translation)

En er   hjartablóð Fáfnis   kom   á tungu hánum,
But the blood of Fáfnir's heart came on tongue his [Sigurðr's],

ok skildi hann   fugls   rödd,
and could him of the bird [understand] the language.

Hann heyrði, at igður klökuðu á hrísinu.
He heard the nuthatches that whispered on the bushes.

[A nuthatch is a small bird, slightly larger than a titmouse, that feeds on worms it finds in the bark of trees. Though much smaller, its beak shape is similar to a woodpecker's and it is very discrete, as opposed to more familiar birds such as a titmouse. We may see in them what we now call the "spirits of the forest," or, in the present context, the Dísir. Their language is certainly as full of magic as the celebrated 'bird language'.]

Igðan kvað:
The nuthatch said:

s. 33	**Literally**	**Translation**
Önnur kvað:	*One said:*	Here is Reginn lying
Þar liggr Reginn,	Here is lying Reginn	calculating for his
ræðr um við sik,	planning for himself,	own interest,
vill tæla mög	he will betray the boy	he will betray the boy
þann er trúir hánum, ...	who relies on him...	who has confidence
	will want the evil-smith	in him,
vill bölvasmiðr (bölva-smiðr)		this evil-doer will
bróður hefna.	a brother to avenge.	want to avenge his
		brother.

Fáfnir, and even Reginn himself, already have informed Sigurðr of the danger he is facing from Reginn and this is now confirmed by the forest spirits: all say to him to be wary of Reginn. He also knows that Reginn is a powerful wizard and that he may have shaped Sigurðr's fates so that they irrevocably lead to his death (Sigurðr's). We can express this, in this case, by saying that Reginn had cast a spell on Sigurðr so that his fate becomes to die after Fáfnir's killing. Sigurðr, however, wards off this spell by stating, or by understanding that he has a way out if he kills Reginn.

s. 39	Literally	Translation
*"Verða-t svá rík **sköp**,*	Will become-not so powerful the **shapings**	The shapings ('sköp') will not be so powerful
at Reginn skyli	that Reginn must	that Reginn must
mitt banorð (ban-orð) bera;	my 'of death-word' [my death sentence] carry;	carry my death sentence;
því at þeir báðir bræðr	because them two brothers	because, soon, the two brothers
skulu bráðliga	soon will travel	will leave this place
fara til heljar heðan."	towards Hel from here.	to travel towards Hel.

He thus cuts Reginn's head and, as the text insists upon, he eats Fáfnir's heart and drinks the blood of the two corpses, "the one of Reginn and the one of Fáfnir." Here is a literal translation of this episode:

Sigurðr hjó höfuð af Regin,   ok þá át han Fáfnis   hjarta ok
Sigurðr cuts the head off Reginn, and then ate him Fáfnir's the heart and

drakk blóð   þeira beggja, Regins ok Fáfnis.
drunk the blood of all two,   Reginn and Fáfnir.

Þá heyrði Sigurðr,   hvar   igður mæltu:
Then heard Sigurðr, what the nuthatches said:

s. 40	Literally	Translation
Bitt þú Sigurðr	Tie Sigurðr	Pack up, Sigurðr,
bauga rauða,	the red rings,	the treasure of red gold rings
er-a konungligt	is-not regal	it is not worthy of a king
kvíða mörgu;	to fear much;	to fear and hesitate so much;
mey veit ek eina	a maid know I single	I know an exceptional maid,
miklu fegrsta,	very most beautiful,	she is full of beauty
gulli gædda,	of gold equipped,	and with gold outfitted,
ef þú geta mættir.	if you obtain meet.	if you are able to obtain her.

After all these events, it is quite possible that Sigurðr was a little hesitant in choosing a best behavior. The 'spirit-nuthatches' call him to order and say that he now has to go to Sigrdrífa, the woman he must meet. Grípir already announced his future and already announced to him the need for this meeting.

In the following stanza, the nuthatches warn him on the fact that awaking her is not an excellent idea.

s. 44	Literally	Translation
Knáttu mögr séa	You know how, boy, to see	You, lad, will be able to see
mey und hjalmi,	the girl under the helmet	the girl under the helmet
þá er frá vígi	when towards the combat	when she rode to combat
Vingskorni reið;	on Vingskornir rode;	on Vingskornir (her horse);
má-at Sigrdrífar	you are able-not Sigrdrífa	Child of Skjöldungr, (son of a great family)
svefni bregða,	of her sleep to split,	you are not able to stop
skjöldunga niðr,	child of Skjöldungr,	Sigrdrífa's sleep
*fyr **sköpum norna**.*	against the **Norns' shapings**.	against the **Norns' shapings**.

Sigrdrífa is a Valkyrie who disobeyed Óðinn's orders by not bringing to Valhöll the warrior he wanted to die in combat. To punish her, he pricks her with "the thorn of sleep." Óðinn, in this case, is who decided of Sigrdrífa's shapings. In this very case again, we could also say that he "cast a spell on her," that he "shaped a spell on her."

The nuthatches say very clearly that Sigurðr will be unable to awake her. When we will see how he awakes her, we will understand that either the 'spirits' were misled, or they wanted to imply that awaking her was very dangerous because he would then find himself overlapping with the Norns's intentions, i.e. he would follow the destiny Grípir has foreseen. This last assumption seems to be the most probable.

In other words, the nuthatches tried to prevent Sigurðr from wakening Sigrdrífa because this would provide him a possibility for escaping his örlög. Obviously, the last is unthinkable and Sigurðr will properly behave (i.e. awaken Sigrdrífa) and this brings him into enduring his örlög.

This may seem somewhat complicated: in the general conclusion we will precise the meaning of *sköp*, a word that can be used pejoratively, or even insultingly, to point at who sends *sköp*.

The following poem is called Sigrdrífu–*mál*, 'of Sigrdrífa–the word', because when she meets Sigurðr she is still a Valkyrie (she will be called Brynhildr later, her best-known name).

II-10. Sigrdrífumál

The poem begins with a comment:

Sigurðr gekk í **skjaldborgina**
Sigurðr entered the **stronghold-shield**
[We may suppose this is a name of a stronghold built in a particular way]

---

ok sá, at þar lá **maðr** *ok svaf með öllum hervápnum.*
and he saw, there was **human person** and (who) was 'quiet' and fully armed.

Hann tók fyrst hjálminn af höfði hánum. **Þá sá hann, at þat var kona.**
He removed first the helmet off her head. Then, he saw that 'it' was a woman.

Brynjan var föst sem hon væri holdgróin.
The coat of arms was tight as if it had grown in the flesh.

Þá reist hann með Gram frá höfuðsmátt brynjuna í gögnum
Then he gashed with Gram from the upper part of the coat of arms gear

---

niðr ok svá út í gögnum báðar ermar.
to down and until the gear of the two arms.

Þá tók hann brynju af henni, en hon vaknaði, ok settist hon upp
Then he took the coat of arms out of her and she woke up, and sat she up

---

ok sá Sigurðr ok mælti …
and saw Sigurðr and said …

Sigrdrífa sleeps in a very particular place, which is a fort bearing the name of a war tactic. Let us note that, when he arrives, Sigurðr sees a fully-armed warrior so that he calls him/her a human person (*maðr*). As the spirits-nuthatches foresaw, he "can see the girl under her helmet:" when meeting her, his first action is to take off her helmet.

Up to that point, he followed the nuthatches advice and he was able to shape the fates in order to keep some control on his destiny. Does he know he will wake her by slicing her coat of arms? At any rate, this coat of arms seems to be grown in the flesh and he can suspect that it will awake the sleeping beauty. Thus, voluntarily or by negligence, and in spite of the nuthatches advice, he will slice this coat and he will wake up Sigrdrífa, and with her, their common örlög.

s.1	Literally
Hvat beit brynju?	What bit the coat of mail?
Hví brá ek svefni?	Why I stopped my sleep?
Hverr felldi af mér	Who fell from me
fölvar nauðir?	the pale needs?

In this context, the "pale needs" evoke the paleness of a corpse-like Sigrdrífa in her bewitched sleep due to Óðinn's shapings.

Thus, Sigurðr awoke Sigrdrífa and their destinies went as far as becoming the Germanic representatives of the pressure destiny can put upon us.

They will passionately love each other and as Grípir said: (s. 29),

"*gára þú manna*	you will not give any more attention to humankind
Nema þú mey séir	nothing except the maid you will see" but remember
	that s. 31 says:
"*It munuð alla*	You two together will want all
eiða vinna	oaths work out
fullfastliga,	fully-firm ones
fá munuð halda.	few will you be able to keep."

II-11. Reginsmál

This poem begins with the well-known myth where Loki buys back his involuntary murder of Hreiðmarr's son, Otr, while he was in the shape of an otter. The three Æsir, Óðinn, Hœnir and Loki, make a bag of his skin. Ignoring the exact nature of this otter, they show the bag to Hreiðmarr, who recognizes the skin of his son and requires a wergild, otherwise he will have to avenge his son. This compensation is enormous (according to the usual standards), it consists in filling the bag with gold, to put it upright on its 'legs' filled up with gold, then to cover it with a gold heap. Loki who killed Otr is in charge to gather the gold, which includes a ring he coveted.

Loki joins the dwarf Andvari (details in the 'tale' 'Nibelung's three Curses') who lives in water in the form of a pike. This last one asserts:

s. 2

"Andvari heiti ek,	Andvari I am called,
Óinn hét minn faðir,	Óinn was my father called,
margan hef ek fors of farit,	by many torrents I travelled,
aumlig norn	a **wretched Norn**
skóp *oss í árdaga,*	**shaped** for us in the old days
at skylda ek í vatni vaða"	thus it occurs that in water I wade.

We know that **skóp** is the preterit of the verb *skapa*, to shape. In this case, the allusion to a fate thrown by a wretched Norn (*aumligr* is a kind of insult!) is denounced by Andvari and the sköp thrown at Andvari by this mysterious Norn shaped him into a pike. This way of speaking shows that Andvari estimates to have undergone an unbearable prejudice.

Since örlög have to be proudly endured, it would be shaming to complain about one's örlög. This is why Andvari, who believes that the örlög he deserved had been twisted, puts responsibility of this change on a 'twisted' Norn, here presented as a commonplace witch who shapes *sköp*.

The nuthatches, Sigurðr's advisers, also speak of Norn's sköp (§ II-9, stanza 44). In the same way, the *"ljótar* **nornir skópu** *langa þrá* (dreadful Norns (who) shaped a long painful desire)" to Brynhildr and Sigurðr (§ II-12, stanza 7) are insulted by Brynhildr.

These ways of speech differ from those relating Norns to örlög creation. For example, in § II-9, stanza 11, Fáfnir prophesies to Sigurðr that he will know *"Norna dóm* (Norns's doom)" which is nothing else than (once again!) to describe his örlög.

We will partly explain these differences when meeting other examples and do it fully in chapter II conclusion.

Once Loki has obtained Andvari's gold, the Æsir can pay the requested wergild. When this is done, Hreiðmarr notices that one otter hair is still visible, which forces Óðinn to hide it with this invaluable ring. Loki thought he had already much given to obtain all this gold and he is exasperated by Hreiðmarr's meanness. Loki will thus utter a curse (called here a string of sköp) onto Hreiðmarr. We know that this curse will take place: Fáfnir, another of Hreiðmarr's sons, will kill his father and seize the treasure … and we already have seen in § II-9 how these sköp will strike again. The wizard, here Loki, who launches sköp has precise reasons (here Hreiðmarr's meanness) for shaping them, and he is able to explain it.

This curse is sent in stanza 6:

Gull er þér nú reitt	Gold is yours now wrathful [the wrathful gold is now yours]
en þú gjöld of hefr	But you compensations increase
mikil míns höfuðs,	much of my head [you increase much the compensations for my head],
syni þínum	for son yours
verðr-a sæla **sköpuð**;	not becomes happy **the shaped**;
þat verðr ykkarr beggja bani.	that becomes of you <u>two both</u> the death.

A curse is intended to modify the destiny of the cursed one. Loki does not try to modify Hreiðmarr's örlög but he requests the forces of sköp in order to influence the course of Hreiðmarr's life. In addition, we also notice that Loki does not give details on the way in which Hreiðmarr and his son will die. On the other hand, Loki makes a point at specifying the reason for which Hreiðmarr's shapings can be modified: he has been unable to be generous when obtaining a generous compensation. This shows that sköp are not randomly thrown: the sorcerer is able to validate his use of sköp.

Hreiðmarr has two more sons: Reginn (name not associated to 'regin', the gods, but to *regi*, cowardice—the Coward), and Fáfnir (meaning dubious, perhaps resulting from *fá-fengr* = catch-booty). Reginn and Fáfnir request of their father their share of the spoils because they took part in the violence made to the Æsir. Facing his father's refusal, "*Fáfnir lagði sverði*

Hreiðmar föður sinn sofanda (Fáfnir put a sword (in) Hreiðmarr, father his, sleeping)" and seizes the spoils. Reginn would like to have also his share and requests it from Fáfnir who refuses. Reginn then asks his sister's advice and she advises him to use softness: "*Bróður kveðja / skaltu blíðliga* ... (your brother in good mood will you ask...)." His sister holds him a coward and, as expected, Reginn does not obtain anything. We also know that Fáfnir will disappear with his treasure while being transformed into a dragon as we saw in Fáfnismál § II-9.

Reginn does not have thus the courage to face a dragon shape-changed brother and he decides to raise a future hero who will be able to achieve this feat: Sigurðr, whose he becomes the adoptive father.

He declares in s. 14:

Ek mun fæða	I will raise
folkdjarfan gram;	the people-proud furious one;
nú er Yngva konr	now is Yngvi's kinsman
með oss kominn;	with us come;
sjá mun ræsir	he will (be) a leader
ríkstr und sólu;	most powerful under the sun;
þrymr um öll lönd	glorious in all lands,
örlögsímu.	**örlög-ropes** [örlög-bound].

[Sigurðr will carry three features: powerful, glorious and 'bound to his örlög']

The neutral substantive *síma* (plural *símu*) 'cord, string', primarily indicates according to its etymology (given by deVries) something that links, constrains, i.e. rather a bow cord than a cord dangling down. We see that this significant image tells of binding Sigurðr to Reginn and that the tension thus created between the two men informs the listeners of the poem recitation that their relation will dramatically end.

Reginn thus wishes to take along Sigurðr to Fáfnir's cave with the intention to recover this famous treasure with which Loki paid his wergild. Sigurðr haughtily refuses. He argues that it would be ridiculous that the prince (him) has more "the desire to seek/red rings (of red gold)/than avenge his father!" They thus go away in order to punish Sigurðr's father killer.

On their way, they meet an old magician, Hnikarr, who will inform Sigurðr of his future as a warrior, as already done by Grípir. This knowledge will be useful in the necessary fights against his father's murderer. Sigurðr requires from Hnikarr the signs, the omens or predictions by which a warrior may foresee the outcome of a battle.

He begins his request by:

s. 19

Segðu mér Hnikarr,	Tell me Hnikarr,
alls þá hvártveggja veizt	all, for both of them, you know
goða **heill** *ok guma: ...*	the **omens** for the gods and humankind…

The substantive *heill* has several meanings. When it is a neutral (as here) it means 'forecasts, predictions'.

Sigurðr undoubtedly follows Hnikarr's invaluable advice because he fights his father's killers and overcomes them. To his father's murderer, he applies the ancient punishment, the one that restores your honor, i.e. death by the 'bloody eagle'.

Sigurðr states:

s. 26

Nú er blóðugr örn	Now is the bloody eagle
bitrum hjörvi	with a biting sword
bana Sigmundar	for the death of Sigmundr (Sigurðr's father)
á baki ristinn...	on the back carved…

The poem uses word *örn* meaning a bird, the eagle. The symbolic value of this execution is so strong because the two lungs spouting out of the back of the victim evoke an emblem also called an eagle, i.e. proclamation that justice has been done.

The poem does not insist on this point, but it is clear that these settings of a ritual death are of extreme importance in the way the hero shapes his life, his *sköp*. This is understood implicitly because, to some extent, Reginn shaped for Sigurðr's a life in which he would kill Fáfnir so that Reginn could finally recover the treasure. Sigurðr thus rebels against Reginn's sköp and shapes himself his own ones. We already met this behavior, much more explicitly expressed in Fáfnismál, (II-9).

Reginn thus takes along Sigurðr towards Fáfnir's cave in order to kill Fáfnir and to get back this obsessing treasure.

II-12. Sigurðarkviða in skamma

This 'short' Ballad is nevertheless 71 stanzas long. It describes how Sigrdrífa, now called Brynhildr, will push her husband (Gunnarr) to organize Sigurðr's murder. At the end of the poem, she describes her own suicide and, during her anguish, she predicts the future of Gunnarr and Sigurðr's widow, Guðrún.

Stanza 5 tells us of a Brynhildr without defects and of a rather pure naivety: destiny is seen as responsible for her death and Sigurðr's.

s. 5

Hon sér at lífi	She led her life
löst né vissi	of a <u>flaw</u> did not know
ok at aldrlagi	and until death
ekki grand,	no guile,
vamm þat er væri	(or) blemish of any kind
eða vera hygði;	to exist she could think of;
gengu þess á milli	went in between that
grimmar urðir.	**stern and ferocious fates.**
	[Orchard: « cruel fates », Boyer: « the cruel Norns »]

Note on the translation: Orchard and Boyer's translation are perfectly 'correct'. We have been here unable to choose between 'cruel' and 'stern'. These two qualifiers are so different that choosing one or the other mutilates the text.

Löstr means 'defect, bad behavior'. It carries no allusion to a Christian 'sin', except perhaps after conversion times.

Stanza 5 is stated by an unbiased witness and he/she uses a classical way of speech to describe the unpleasant sides of our örlög. Here, typically, a translation that does not take into account the Norse worldview may lead to a complete misunderstanding of the poem.

Adjective *grimmr* is certainly not a laudatory one. In this stanza, though, the story teller expresses a well-known fact, his/her speech carries no hate towards Norns. We will, below, meet a desperate Brynhildr, herself furious at the Norns in a way similar to dwarf Andvari in § II-11.

These 'stern and ferocious' fates explain why, in stanza 6, Brynhildr's heart and body flare up and she declares:

s. 6

"*Hafa skal ek Sigurð,*	I have to get Sigurðr
–eða þó svelta,	–or yet die/kill."

Verb *svelta* means both to die and to kill and she indeed is starting the process by which they will both die.

Moreover, she at once regrets the words she just uttered ... but she will go on enduring her destiny, while blaming the Norns for the misfortunes-sköp they sent upon her, as stanza 7 shows:

s. 7

Orð mæltak nú,	A word I uttered now,
iðrumk eptir þess:	I will be sorry later of it:
kván er hans Guðrún,	his wife is Guðrún,
en ek Gunnars;	and I Gunnarr's;
ljótar nornir	**wretched Norns**
	[Orchard: « **contrary Norns** », Boyer: « The **ugly Norns** »]
skópu <u>oss</u> *langa þrá.*	**shaped** <u>for us</u> a lengthy painful yearning.
	[Orchard: « **pitched** <u>us</u> », Boyer: « **caused** <u>to us</u> »]

In principle, Norns, as divinities, write the destinies and they do not throw curses that will reshape the destinies. We already have met, in § II-11, Dwarf Andvari who qualifies a Norn as 'wretched'. The two cases have in common a sharp resentment against Norns. It follows that the explanation in § II-11 applies also here: Brynhildr does not dare complaining of her örlög though she is unable to refrain from cursing Norns, which does not seem as shameful as whining at one's örlög.

Another fact will interact with a deep understanding of Brynhildr's behavior. She knows that a woman, Grímhildr, did shape her destiny and that herself and Gudrún also contributed to her fate.

It is thus possible to see here a double meaning for word *nornir*: on the one hand, the Norns themselves (when they wrote her destiny) and on the other one, a *heiti* for 'women' who would be then these "wretched women-Norns" responsible for the chaotic course of her life.

For better knowing Brynhildr's and Grímhildr's traits, we need exposing the two versions of Grímhildr's poisoning history, one told by Völsunga saga, the other by poetic Edda, in particular stanzas 21-26 of Guðrúnarkviða in forna.

Interlude

Magic drinks used in Völsunga saga and Guðrúnarkviða in forna

- Völsunga saga version

As the preceding poems taught us, Völsunga saga says how Sigurðr released Brynhildr (ex-Sigrdrífa) off Óðinn's shapings. Sigurðr expresses his desire to take Brynhildr as wife:

"*þess sver ek við guðin, at ek skal þik eiga eða enga konu ella*

I oath near the gods, that I will you 'possess' (to marry) and not a different woman"

says Sigurðr, and the saga adds:

"*Hún mælti slíkt*

She spoke in the same way."

From our point of view, the one of the comprehension of destinies, three women will decide of Sigurðr's destiny: Brynhildr herself, of course, but also Grímhildr and Guðrún. Grímhildr is the wife of the king with whom Sigurðr decided to live (Gunnarr), and she is Guðrún's mother. The saga describes her as being "*fjölkunnga* (very-knowing, witch)" and "*grimmhuguð kona* (stern ferocious spirited woman)." When this beautiful warrior appears, fantastically wealthy from Fáfnir's recovered treasure, she decides that he will marry her daughter Guðrún. She is quite conscious of the bonds linking Brynhildr and Sigurðr and she nevertheless uses her magic by making him drink a potion of memory loss, so that he forgets his promises. The saga says simply that she makes him drink this potion without giving details on its composition.

- *Guðrúnarkviða in forna version*

Among the poems dealing with this topic, the only one explaining why Sigurðr forgets his oaths to Brynhildr is found in Grípisspá s. 33:

> "*Þú verðr, siklingr,* You will become, young prince,
> *fyr* **svikum** *annars,* by other **treacheries-poisons**,
> *muntu Grímhildar* you will from Grímhildr
> *gjalda ráða.*" suffer the counsels.

When a translator forgets the meaning 'poison' for *svik* as does Boyer: "treasons", and Orchard: "plots", the reader has to imagine by her/himself the existence of a bond between the Völsunga saga poisoned drink and Grípisspá s. 33. However, *svik* carries both meanings of treason and poison, i.e. one should translate it here by "treacherous poison", for example. This explains how Grímhildr, in Völsunga saga, has been able to 'force' Sigurðr to forget his oath to Brynhildr.

We will see in Guðrúnarkviða in forna below (§ II-14) that Grímhildr again uses a forgetting potion, now on Guðrún, in order to make her forget her sorrow after Sigurðr's death and to push her to marry another king. In this case, the magic process is described in some details.

All things considered, the conjunction of Völsunga saga and poetic Edda indicates that Grímhildr used twice a magic potion for memory lapse, which makes of her a dangerous witch. By her charms, she is able to shape the fate of her close parents, and this is what comes out of stanzas 5 and 7 of Sigurðarkviða in skamma.

We now will study stanza 58 that confirms all these assumptions. During her death throes, Brynhildr pronounces several prophecies related to Gunnarr and she besides interprets in an interesting way the failure of their relation in last two lines of the stanza:

58.

Muntu Oddrúnu	You will Oddrún
eiga vilja,	own wish, (you will wish to marry Oddrún)
en þik Atli	though to you Atli
mun eigi láta;	will not let (Atli will not agree to your relationship);

it munuð lúta	both will you lower yourselves (agree to)
á laun saman,	in secret together (meet in secret),
hon mun þér unna,	she will to you give love
sem ek skyldak,	as I should have
ef okkr góð of **sköp**	if to us good (magic) **shapings**
gerði verða.	**would have been brought.**

Oddrún is the sister of Atli (who corresponds to the historical character Attila).

The verb **verða**, to become, is the verb plural preterit of which is *urðu*, associated to Norn Urðr.

The last two lines indicate that Brynhildr does not attribute to an immutable örlög the failure of her relation with Gunnarr but to 'bad shapings' (bad sköp), that were thrown at them, as if her and Sigurðr had been simple human ones and not heroes tightly fitted around their örlög. The interlude above describes how these bad spells have been cast.

71.

Mart sagða ek,	Much could I say,
munda ek fleira,	would I have more,
	(I could have said much more)
er mér meir **mjötuðr**	if for me **mjötuðr** ('measure-supplier')
málrúm gæfi;	word-place (time for other words) gave me;
ómun þverr,	the voice dies out,
undir svella,	under (the effect of) swelling,
satt eitt sagðak,	truth one (the very truth) I declared (about me–I truly described myself)
svá mun ek láta.	thus I will let go.

We already saw that *mjötuðr* is the 'measurer' who allots the measure of everything, as would be the conductor of a spiritual orchestra. According to the context, it will mean, in Norse either (optimistic view) a god, a guard, or (pessimistic view) a plague. Thus, this word points at an organizer who can be either favorable or unfavorable.

The commentators were deeply influenced by an Anglo-Saxon related word: *meotud* or *metod* which means 'destiny, creator, God, Christ'. In this language, *metod* represents only the optimistic side of the measure giver. The simultaneously negative aspect present in ON *mjötuðr* is rendered, in Anglo-Saxon, by another word *metodsceaft*: 'creation/construction of *metod*' which means 'decree of the destiny, doom, death'.

Conclusion

Brynhildr's words suggest that she does not consider that her split from Sigurðr has been registered on Norns engraved, immutable small wooden planks. She deems that she underwent two sköp. The first has been inflicted by Óðinn for her rebellion, of which she does not violently complain since it led her to meet Sigurðr. For the second one, as we have now seen, she bitterly complains of Grímhildr's *sköp* because it enables her to avoid cursing her örlög that obviously included her split from Sigurðr.

Brynhildr was herself a powerful magician, and by teaching runes to Sigurðr, as described by Sigrdrífumál, she believed to have forged some *sköp* that would forever bind them. She is obviously wounded as a magician and as a loving woman, and also as an ON person who values the ethic worth of sworn oaths. She says to Gunnarr that she despises him because he is an oath breaker, which shows that she must think the same of her Sigurðr: he certainly is the most courageous warrior (as opposed to Gunnarr), but he is also an oath breaker, though an unintentional one since Grímhildr tricked him. Lastly, she realizes that Grímhildr was a more powerful magician than her since she struck at the weaker link, that is Sigurðr who certainly deemed Guðrún quite an attractive young woman … and thus Grímhildr's task at splitting their couple has been eased.

This battle of magicians between Brynhildr and Grímhildr is implicit in the texts, and we hope to have clarified the circumstances of their lives that illustrate that Brynhildr's örlög have certainly not included a happy life with Sigurðr.

Let us now come back to more down to earth sections of this fight.

II-13. Guðrúnarkviða in fyrsta

This poem describes Guðrún's suffering when she discovers Sigurðr's body. It starts with a prose comment.

"*Guðrún sat to yfir Sigurdhi dauðum ...*
Guðrún sat for Sigurðr's corpse ...
hon var búinn til at springa af harmi.
she was about to burst with sadness.
Til gengu bæði konur ok karlar at hugga hana,
To her went both women and men to take care of her,
in þat var eigi auðvelt.
but that was not easy."

In particular, her sister Gullrönd tries to comfort her by asking her to kiss the corpse's lips and, actually, Guðrún's pain intensifies. She ends up insulting Brynhildr calling her "*armrar vættar* (malicious soul, here = essence of wickedness)." This last one is nearby and she answers, which causes Gullrönd's fury and she shouts at her as follows:

24.

Þá kvað þat Gullrönd	Thus Gullrönd spoke,
Gjúka dóttir:	Gjúki's daughter girl:
"*Þegi þú, þjóðleið,*	"Be silent, very-hateful one,
þeira orða;	of these words;
	(do not utter, very hateful one, these words)
urðr *öðlinga*	the **fate** (here: an unhappy one, death) of princes
hefr þú æ verit,	you always have been;
rekr þik alda hver	you unfold to these people
illrar **skepnu**,	a bad a shape/fate/'**shaping**',
sorg sára	(you have been) a sorrow wound
sjau konunga	to seven kings
ok vinspell	and friendship-destruction
vífa mest."	of women the largest."
	(the biggest destroyer of friendship between women)

Skepnu is also related to the verb *skapa*, to shape, and means here a shaping, as a singular form for *sköp*. Here, Brynhildr is accused to have shaped evil on 'these people'. Since we know that she taught magic to Sigurðr, accusing her of magic behavior is certainly justified, though all we know reduces to our hypothesis of a magic fight between her and Grímhildr in the 'interlude' of § II-12.

II-14. Guðrúnarkviða in forna

This poem is interesting because it explains how Grímhildr's *sköp* have been concocted, her shapings.

21.

Forði mér Grímhildr	Brought to me Grímhildr
full at drekka	a full (horn) for drinking
svalt ok sárligt,	cold and wounding,
né ek sakar munðak;	not I to blame could
	(I could no more blame something)
þat var of aukit	it was enhanced
jarðar magni,	by earth power,
	(Hávamál 137 quotes as well "earth power"
	and the role of a corn-ear in magic.)
svalköldum sæ	by cold and frozen sea
ok sónum dreyra.	and by a porcine-sacrificial blood
	(blood of a sacrificial pig).

22.

Váru í horni	Were (written) on the horn
hvers kyns stafir	any kind of magic signs
ristnir ok roðnir,	carved and (blood-)reddened
–ráða ek né máttak;	–to read (them) I could not;
lyngfiskr langr,	heather-fish (serpent) long,
lands Haddingja	of Haddings' country
ax óskorit,	a corn ear unmarked (not carved, intact),
innleið dyra (dýra).	bowels of a beast (any animal except a bird).

23.

Váru þeim bjóri	Were there in the beer
böl mörg saman,	many evils together,
urt alls viðar	roots of all trees

ok akarn brunnin,	and of acorns roasted,
umdögg arins,	around-dew of hearth (= soot)
iðrar blótnar,	entrails (coming from a) blót, (religious sacrifice)
svíns lifr soðin,	of a pig the boiled liver,
því at hon sakar deyfði.	with that the pains soothed.

[We know of a family of heroes, the Haddingjar, we however know nothing of their exact localization. Boyer states "the country of dead ones" and Orchard, "the sea" without real justification. Grímhildr's goal is double, blunting Guðrún's pain and making her forget Sigurðr's death.]

It is obvious that we do not understand anymore the magic recipes of old. But, as long as *sköp* are so present in skaldic poetry, they should have been extremely important. Here, it is enough to convince the reader that *sköp* are the methods used by the magicians who try reshaping örlög. In a sense, örlög are fate 'raw material', and *sköp* are the result after a wizard-artist left his/her trace on them, as a piece of furniture testifies the skill of a craftsman at shaping wood.

II-15. Oddrúnarkviða (*or* Oddrúnargrátr)

In this poem, Oddrún describes her misfortunes. She is Atli's and Brynhildr's sister. The three of them are king Budli's children

s. 16

En hann Brynhildi	And he (Budli) for Brynhildr
bað hjalm geta,	begged (asked) the helmet to obtain,
hana kvað hann óskmey	she said that she wish-maiden (Valkyrie)
verða skyldu;	to become wanted;
	Budli requested that Brynhildr could become a warrior. On her side, she wished to become a Valkyrie.
kvað-a hann ina æðri	(she) that said that she highest
<u>alna</u> *(gen. plur.) mundu*	of the '<u>measures</u>' should

mey (acc.) í heimi,	maiden in the house (the world), (she said that she was to become the highest maid reference in the world)
nema **mjötuðr** *spillti.*	unless the **giver of measure** would waste (all that).

This stanza uses the word 'alna' genitive plural of *alin*, the length of a forearm, or any measurement. *Mjöt* is also a measure, and it is impossible that the skald could have been unaware of it: he plays with *alin* and *mjötuðr*. We can thus see here a pun on Brynhildr's 'measure' and the one used by the universal measure giver.

We have seen, in Sigurðarkviða in skamma § II-12, a similar way of speech where everything is perfect until "**grimmar urðir**" come into play. It is thus clear that this *mjötuðr* is here a form of *urðr*, of destiny.

Recall that the word *mjötuðr* is used in Sigurðarkviða in skamma s. 71, also with a meaning similar to *urðr*.

The last stanza concludes:

34.

Sattu ok hlýddir,	You had sat and listened
meðan ek sagðak þér	while I told you
mörg ill of **sköp**	much evil of the **shapings**
mín ok þeira;	mine and theirs; (I said much evil of mine and the others' shapings)
maðr hverr lifir	human being each lives
at munum sínum.	with duties his.
Nú er of genginn	Now is gone (ended)
grátr Oddrúnar.	the wailing of Oddrún.

Thus, the two sisters, Brynhildr and Oddrún speak of the *sköp* they devised on themselves and others 'since' even heroes and gods do not deal with örlög.

II-16. **Atlakviða** *Dauði Atla*

Guðrún (now, Sigurðr's widow) eventually marries Atli, as her mother wished. This poem, as well as the following, describes how Atli kills Guðrún's brothers, and how the latter are avenged. In stanza 39, we are reaching the outcome, and Guðrún in a fury takes part in the fight.

39.

Gulli söri	Gold she sowed
in gaglbjarta,	the shining-goose,
	[in these times geese were not yet stupid!]
hringum rauðum	with the red rings
reifði hon húskarla;	untied them servants;
sköp *lét hon vaxa*	**sköp** let them swell, grow,
en skíran málm vaða,	and the pure metal 'wade' (stride),
æva fljóð ekki	never the torrent (Guðrún, as a torrent) ever
gáði fjarghúsa.	was concerned with the large house.

She sprinkles with gold the servants of the house so that they join her in battle and she lets the shapings take power upon the participants in this battle, i.e. she boundlessly uses her magic and her gold to fight the enemy.

II-17. Atlamál in grænlenzku

In the first stanza, we understand that Atli's warriors meet to debate about the situation and it follows that

s. 2

Sköp *ærtu skjöldunga*	**Sköp** they let grow 'those of the shield' (Skjöldungs, warriors)
–skyldu-at feigir,–	–should not have been strange/near-death/mad,–
illa réðsk Atla,	badly has been advised Atli,
átti hann þó hyggju;	he had though quite a good mind;

Thus, the warriors, just as Guðrún does in Atlakviða above, cause a 'swell' of the *sköp* i.e. here, the warriors try to shape fate in order to cause a battle. In modern language, one would say that they "increase pressure" but this removes the magic hinted at in this stanza.

Högni and his brothers have been invited to meet Atli in his castle. Guðrún, his wife (and Högni's and Gunnarr's sister), who attended or spied upon the warriors' ceremonies, know that this is a trap. She thus sends a message in runes to warn her brothers but the messenger scrambles the runes. Another woman notices that these runes were tampered with and she tries to warn the guests, with no success. Moreover, Högni shows such an arrogance that he cannot change his mind unless being called a coward. At departure time, Högni and his wife exchange a long glance by which they, a last time, share their love:

36.

Sásk til síðan,	They then looked at each other
áðr í sundr hyrfi,	already separately 'rotated' (taking opposite ways)
*þá hygg ek **sköp** skiptu,*	thus I think the **sköp** had appointed them
skilðusk vegir þeira.	their ways were branching off.

When her brothers appear, Guðrún is afflicted to see that her try at warning them had failed.

48.

Leitaða ek í líkna	I sought a way out
at letja ykkr heiman,	to let you at home
***sköpum** viðr manngi,*	**sköp** against nobody,
ok skuluð þó hér komnir.	and it happens nevertheless that you came.

The *sköp* named in s. 36 and 48 are those about which s. 2 speaks: the ones that will push Atli's warriors to fight to death Guðrún's brothers.

The battle rages and Guðrún's brothers are submerged by the mass of their opponents. The battlefield is flooded with blood.

s. 53

…flóði völlr blóði,	… blood flooded the (battle) field,
átján áðr fellu,	eighteen already fell,
*efri þeir **urðu** …*	the best of them **'became'** (the best warriors **died**).

We meet an unexpected way (for our time) to use verb *verða*, to become. The context clearly announces that they died, thus 'to become' seems not appropriate. We can suppose, as most commentators do, that it takes here the meaning: 'to become what we all must become, i.e. a corpse'.

The following stanza provides some information on the concept of destiny. It is an example of a very ambiguous use of the word 'auðna, chance'.

Atli and Guðrún quarrel one last time during Atli's death anguish, she has wounded him to death. Atli tries to justify himself by telling a part of his youth. He and his sisters (we suppose so), following Sigurðr, wandered on the sea:

98.

Þrjú várum systkin,	Three we were, brothers and sisters
	((?) Oddrún, Atli and Brynhildr)
skæva vér létum,	To stride we 'let go',
skipi hvert várt stýrði,	on a ship driven by,
*örkuðum at **auðnu**,*	unknown to **chance/fate**
	(led by an unknown chance/fate),
unz vér austr kvómum.	until we in the East reached.

The word *auðna* appears only once in poetic Edda, it means 'luck', understood as bringing rewards. A ship driven by an unknown luck can, indeed, evoke a ship the course of which is subjected to fate. An anachronistic translation would as much make sense: "our ship followed a random trajectory (and by a fortunate coincidence we arrived in the East)." This is why we may understand that *auðna* can evoke such luck that carries a meaning similar to the one in "to try one's luck", possibly with very little hope of success, as those who play games of luck.

II-18. Grógaldr

This poem may be somewhat hard to spot. Grógaldr and Fjölsvinnsmál (see next §) were joined together by Bugge under the name of Svipdagsmál, (Bugge, 1867, http://etext.old.no/Bugge/). Some editors may not follow this convention.

Gróa's son, called Svipdagr ('Changing-day'), calls upon his dead mother's assistance because he was put in charge of an impossible mission by his mother-in-law.

4. *Gróa kvað*	4. Gróa said
Löng er för,	Long is the journey
Langir ro farvegar,	long are the ways,
Langir ro manna munir;	long are the wishes/delights of humankind;
ef þat verðr,	if that may be,
at þú þinn vilja bíðr,	with you to your goodwill (genitive) preserve
	(you keep for you the goodwill)
ok skeikar þá	and that then (she) twists (to your advantage)
	(Skuld then twists in your favor)
Skuld / Skuldar at **sköpum.**	Skuld [nominative] by the **sköp**.
	(*or* if *skuldar*, preserve Skuld's [genitive] favor and may her shape thus your fate.)

Verb *bíða*, 'to remain, support, preserve', has its direct object in the genitive, hence the form *vilja*, genitive of *vili*, favor, delight.

The possible choice *Skuldar* (gen. sing.) instead of *Skuld* provides "Skuld's favor." This would lead to the translation: "you preserve 'upon you' Skuld's favor and that then she modifies by *sköp*." Both translations are somewhat strange and we can suppose that this is a ritual formula stating "if possible, preserve Skuld's favor and may her shape thus your fate." In any case, Skuld is not called upon to modify Gróa's son örlög, but to shape them favorably, understating that they could have been also shaped for the worse.

Word *skuld* means debt, which is not something to deal lightly with: It has to be refunded at any price. If we connect Skuld to verb *skulu*, 'must', and its past forms *skyldi* and *skyldu*, we then lightly connect it to the past. The word *skuld*, however, is not at all connected to temporality: a debt is contracted in the past, we pay it in the present or the future. She is thus Norn of debts' refunding, not the one of past times. We do not know the details of the debt Svigþaðr must pay, except that he complains of it in stanza 3, Skuld is thus in proper place here as suggested by our discussion on Norns' names in § I-1.4.

In order to comply to her son's request, Gróa utters/sings nine incantations, while standing on a stone stuck in the ground at the edge of the dead's dwelling … magic can hardly be absent here! The second incantation is:

7.

Þann gel ek þér annan,	Thus I shout/sing a second one,
ef þú árna skalt	if you receive will
viljalauss á vegum:	bad luck on the ways
Urðar *lokur*	(may) **Urðr's** bonds
haldi þér öllum megum,	hold for you the whole strength,
er þú á sinnum sér.	that you (may) in (good) company
	(*or* on a good way) be.

The expression *á sinnum* has also a fixed meaning "on the way (and until its end)."

Remember that word *urðr* is one of the Norse words meaning destiny, as *örlög* and *sköp* among others. As seen in § I-1.4, she draws up the assessment of all our actions. Urðr's bonds must thus refer to the life assessment of Svipdagr. Gróa requests of Urðr that no force can split Svipdagr from his past, so that he may overcome his ordeal.

II-19. Fjölsvinnsmál

As noticed by Bugge, this poem looks like a continuation of the one before. However, in this second poem, the hero is initially presented under the name of Vindkaldr (Wind-Frozen). Only at the end of the poem he will say that he is called Svipdagr, as in Grógaldr. If Bugge's assumption is exact, we could then confuse Svipdagr and Óðr, Freyja's husband, who left her for reasons unknown, we only know that she cried gold tears at his departure [These details are provided here because, in the translations, we see Vindkaldr popping out of nothing and mysteriously disappearing at once].

Freyja is called Menglöð in this poem, Svipdagr-Vindkaldr approaches her dwelling. He meets an unpleasant reception from the guard who says to him that he has nothing to do here. They at first insult each other by both calling the other one a troll ("*Hvat er þat flagða?* 'Who is this troll?')," then the guardian adds "*ok dríf þú nú vargr at vegi.* (and you wipe out now, wolf/monster, toward your way)." These kindnesses being said, they can shift towards serious things and here begins a competition in knowledge. Vindkaldr-Svipdagr asks to the guard questions relating to mythology. As we see, the newcomer is the one who actually puts to test the guardian. This ends when he asks a question that only Svipdagr can ask–just as Óðinn raises a last question by which he reveals his identity in Vafþrúðnismál.

In this case, the loser seems quite happy to have lost the contest, he only is a bit concerned by the possibility of an error: he wisely fears Freyja's wrath in case the newcomer is not Svipdagr.

One of the questions Vindkaldr asks the guardian is relative to the name of the dogs that control also the entrance of the place. The guardian is at first a little scorning ("if you want that knowledge…") but he ends up providing an interesting information. The role of the dogs is to protect the eleven Freyja's maids "*unz rjúfask reginn* (until the gods break)," that is until Ragnarök. In this sentence, rök is paraphrased by 'break'.

14.	The guardian said:
Gífr heitir annarr,	Gífr is called one
en Geri annarr,	and Geri the other,
ef þú vilt þat vita;	if you want that to know;
varðir ellifu	guards to the eleven ones (they are guardians for eleven ones)
er þeir varða,	that protect them, (and they protect Freyja's servants)
*unz **rjúfask regin**.*	until the **gods break**. (until the gods break down.)

Another question raised by Vindkaldr is related to Yggdrasill. The whole exchange explains us why Yggdrasill is also called: "*mjötuðr*," measure-supplier, a word that has nothing in common with the word 'tree'. The guard explains him that Yggdrasill's fruits (possibly yew berries) help during a difficult childbirth [5] and this is why Yggdrasill is human ones' "measure-supplier."

******* A note on "*varðir ellifu*" *******

In 'För Skírnis' s. 19, Skírnir proposes to Gerðr a tremendous gift in order to drive her to answer Freyr's love: She may become the guardian the Æsir's eternal life (as later Íðunn will be). Here is his way to propose this gift:

Epli ellifo	Apples, eleven of them
hér hefi ec algullin,	I have here, all golden,
þá mun ec þér, Gerðr! gefa,	will be to you, Gerðr! given
frið at kaupa,	so as peace buying,
at þú þér Frey kveðir	and that you may say of Freyr
óleiðastan lifa.	(that) non–very-hateful to live.

These eleven apples have been changed into "*Epli ellilyfs* (Apples eleven for long life)" in Dronke's (1997) edition of this poem, with an explanation given p. 407. This explanation comes from s. 9 of a Þjóðólfr úr Hvíni's poem (~ 855–930), called Haustlöng. The poet uses here a kenning to speak of Íðunn as "the young girl who knows the long-life herbs of youth of the Æsir (*mey þás kunni ellilyf ása*)." This provides some information on the kind of magic used in order to avoid aging among Æsir.

We meet here a third time number 11 that seems to be linked to protection in a way we cannot explain.

22.

Út af hans aldni	Since its fruits
skal á eld bera	will be in the fire carried
fyr kelisjúkar [5] konur;	for women in labor;
útar hverfa	outside to turn what
þats þær innar skyli,	to them inside should,
sá er hann með mönnum	from this he is the **measure-supplier** for
mjötuðr.	human ones.

From the point of view of mythology, this denomination is also very interesting. It shows that some 'objects', such as Yggdrasill and Óðrœrir, have a soul as the poet Lamartine says [*Milly ou la terre natale*, 1830] and that, in exceptional circumstances, they can play a direct role. We will meet this phenomenon with Óðrœrir in Hrafnagaldr stanza 2 below.

Lastly, Svipdagr, who has just won his knowledge duel (in a way a 'hypocrite' one, as one often said of Óðinn) provides his name. The last three lines are famous since they clearly state that örlög is not likely to be modified under any pretext. The *sköp* really do not modify it, as already stated, but they shape what is not yet decided in it. For example, death is obviously part of everyone's örlög though the how or when of it is not always fixed in our örlög.

47.

Svipdagr ek heiti,	Svipdagr (Swift-day) I am called
Sólbjart hét minn faðir,	Sólbjart (Sun-brilliance) was called my father,
þaðan rákumz (as given by Rask. Bugge proposes ráumk)	from there led us
vindar kalda vegu;	winds by a frozen way;
Urðar orði	of Urðr the word
kveðr engi maðr,	says/sings/challenges no man,
þótt þat sé við löst lagit.	although this one (word) with error may be kept.

against Urðr's word no one speaks/ sings even if this word is laid by mistake.

The verb *reka*, to lead, does *ráku* in the plural preterit; this is why we preferred Rask's reading of this word.

The verbs *kveðja* and *kveða* both do *kveðr* in the indicative third person singular. *Kveðja* can mean 'to challenge'. *Kveða* means to say/sing. The idea of 'singing' evokes an attempt to oppose örlög by magic.[5]

---

[5] On *bays of yew*: It is not impossible that the ON people noticed that bays of yew or their flesh (not poisonous) alone helped uterus dilatation.

On *kélisjúkr*: This word is translated as 'hysterical' by CV., 'sickly' by deVries. It is clear, according to lines 4 and 5, that all this is about a difficult childbirth which, indeed, can make women insane with pain, but which (since only approximately a century in our civilization) has nothing to do with hysteria nor a morbid temperament. Moreover, LexPoet precisely gives: "*utero laborantes feminæ* (uterus of a woman in labor)", we see how much it was difficult to introduce differently than in Latin this perfectly natural topic.

II-20. Hrafnagaldur Óðins (galdr of Óðinn's ravens)

An online commented translation is available
See bibliography

Stanza 2

Lassen's ON version	YK's literal translation	Lassen's English translation
Ætlun Æsir	Guessed the Æsir	[But] the Æsir divined
alla gátu,	of (some) ill purpose,	the whole plan,
verp*ir* viltu	twisters disturbed	the unpredictable ones caused muddle
vættar rúnum.	the Wights with runes;	with the god's runes (or secrets).
Oðhrærer skylde	Óðhrærir should	Óðhrærir had to
Urdar gejma,	**Urðr** watch,	look after Urður (fate),
mattkat veria	**powerless was (she) to protect**	he could not protect [her]
mest-um þo*r*ra.	from the worse winter (Ragnarök).	from the greater part [of the plan].

This poem describes the moments preceding Ragnarök (also called 'worst winter') and, in addition, it refers to little or unknown myths so that its interpretation is awkward.

Urðr is seen here as representing the gods' destiny. The poem seems to suggest that Ragnarök occurs following a falsification of örlög, which is Norn written and thus Urðr's power itself is falsified.

We may suppose that the author of the poem wanted to refer to the other magic forces which are the **sköp**. All our mythology seems to indicate that, in fact, the örlög of the universe and of our gods announce an inevitable doom that will upset our universe. However, nothing says when nor how this catastrophe will happen. The supernatural entities that the poem names '*verpir*' (my 'twisters' and Lassen's 'unpredictable ones') will, according to this book interpretation, use their runes and, according to Lassen, modify Óðinn's runes in order to obtain the magic shapings, the **sköp**, which will enable Ragnarök to take place on 'the morrow' according to the process described by Völuspá stanzas 40-58. In this case, Norns (represented by Urðr) are too much weakened to go on managing the gods' örlög that 'slips between their fingers' because their runes are falsified.

II-21. Conclusion of Chapter II

First of all, since we are going to speak of various forms of 'destiny' in the ON world, it is desirable to know what is understood by 'destiny' in modern English. If not, we will discuss on the basis a multitude of "For me, destiny is …" and it will be impossible to compare that with örlög, with Norns' magic, rök etc.

Here are two traditional definitions of destiny. Webster's: "seemly inevitable or necessary succession of events. What will necessarily happen to any person or thing; (one's) fate. That which determines events: said of either a super natural agency or necessity;" Littré: "the sequence of the things regarded as necessary." In addition, we all know that in everyday language, we tend to call past örlög: 'stories' or 'history' and to reduce örlög or destiny to the unknown future aspects of a living creature or thing.

In every day definitions, the temporal aspect of "the succession of events" is not clarified. Indeed, we can very well speak in the past tense of the destiny of a character (preferably a famous and deceased one) and speak of the future destiny of a living character. Especially in the commonplace definition, it would be awkward to speak of the past destiny of an alive character. On the contrary, in old Norse culture, we have seen that it is usual to speak of past örlög which implicitly though relentlessly recalls how much past and future örlög are linked together. In the same register of ideas, the majority of our cultural examples of destiny describe a person as being headlong opposed to the achievement of his/her destiny as long it has not been concocted by him/herself. This is not really the case in poetic Edda. When an allusion is made to the reaction of an individual to his/her destiny, he/she is rather advised to subject oneself to it and to be (perhaps implicitly) full of pride for his/her behavior.

This is why we often did not translate the words *örlög, sköp, rök, mjötuðr* uniformly by 'destiny' while hoping that the context helps the reader to understand that they are more complex forces than the ones of our modern destiny.

On Norns and their magic

We could note that poetic Edda provides seven allusions to the Norns' magic capacities.

- Völuspá stanza 20 says that "they scrape on small planks human ones' örlög" –which hints at them <u>stating</u> these örlög.
- Fáfnismál stanza 11 speaks of "*Norna dóm* (Norns's doom)" i.e. of their capacity to bring doom into a human destiny.
- Conversely, Hrafnagaldur Óðins stanza 2 declares that Norn Urðr, because of an interference of 'twisters', *mattkat* ('non-has-capacity, fails') to protect humankind from the famous "worse winter" that announces Ragnarök, which suggests that she holds, during normal times, a role in humankind's protection.

These three examples describe Norns' magic capacity to manage human destinies in general, in favor of or against humankind, which confirms the traditional Norns's role and looks like our 'destiny'. Nevertheless, in the four following examples, they seem to be interested in individual destinies, apparently in the same way as a human wizard.

- in Fáfnismál stanza 44, the nuthatches who warned Sigurðr of Reginn's threat, prophesy (wrongly) Sigurðr's incapacity to wake up Sigrdrífa, which would have turned him away from "Norn's *sköp*." That the nuthatches might have been mistaken is of no importance, but this way of speech implies that, in this case, the *sköp* were shaped by Norns rather than by a human person or by another divinity.
- In Reginsmál s. 2, dwarf Andvari insults an "*aumlig* (wretched)" Norn who **skóp** (shaped) him into a pike.
- In Grógaldr s. 4, Gróa wishes her son to be protected from misfortune by Skuld's *sköp*.
- In Sigurðarkviða in skamma s. 44, Brynhildr also complains about *ljótar nornir* (dreadful Norns) who *skópu* (shaped) for her and Sigurðr a "long painful desire." She complains they have been deprived of the fulfillment of their desire, of which she has been painfully conscious. Her way of speech, "long painful desire" expresses a suffering quite different from the one of the languor of a 19th century deserted heroine.

Being deprived of one's passion seems to have been placed very high in the Norse torture scale, as unveiled by Grímnismál s. 20.

* * *

Digression 1 about a link between Óðinn and Muninn

While studying the roles of Óðinn's two ravens as presented in 'Huginn and Muninn', we argued that the meaning of the name Muninn is not "memory" as usually stated but it rather means 'passion' as suggested by one of the meanings of *munr* (passion). Most commentators insist on it meaning 'memory' but this does not fit the main stream of its many meanings. Note also that Dronke (2011, her translation of Grímnismál, p. 116) very aptly calls it 'Heart' which is in the same line as 'passion'. Here is Grímnismál s. 20:

Huginn ok Muninn	Huginn and Muninn (Dronke: **Mind and Heart**)
fljúga hverjan dag	fly each day
Jörmungrund yfir;	over Jörmungrund (here 'the earth');
óumk (verb óa) ek of Hugin	fear I for Huginn
at hann aftr (aptr) né komit,	that he back does not come
þó sjámk meir um Muninn.	though "(I) terrify me" for Muninn.

We understand that Óðinn deems it much more harmful to lose his passion (or Heart) than losing his intelligence. We can then guess that Brynhildr's complaint, a seemingly slightly sentimental one, actually expresses a real torturing for an ancient Norse warrior.

These examples seem to imply that Norns can practice the same magic as human persons and gods, i.e. the one of *sköp*. Examining the contexts in which they seem able to play their main role, that is figuring örlög, we will note three possible explanations to this kind of 'deviation'.

The first consists in supposing that the word 'norn' is a heiti pointing at particularly powerful sorceress. This would undoubtedly be possible for Grímhildr in Sigurðarkviða in skamma, who played such an active role in Sigurðr's and Brynhildr's life course but does not fit the three other cases.

The second is to understand that *sköp* turn often to be curses, and that cursed ones react by insulting the cursing ones. To speak about the *sköp* of a

Norn amounts calling her a 'cheap witch', as way of expressing one's anger. This way of speaking enables the speaker to avoid the shame of vilifying his/her own örlög, that makes of us 'true human ones', therefore avoiding self-debasing.

The third amounts to hypothesizing that some especially important characters bear such highly significant örlög that the *sköp* sent to them cannot but bring them back on the way traced by their örlög. The French poet La Fontaine, in *L'Horoscope*, inspired by an Aesop's Fable (which suggests a possible Sumerian influence), nicely expressed this ancient knowledge, classically illustrated by Oedipus' fate: "We meet our destiny/Often on the ways by which we try to avoid it …" In this case, örlög and *sköp* intermingle so much that it is impossible to make a difference between them. In the examples met here, Sigurðr and Brynhildr are first-size human heroes, Svigpadr certainly is Freyja's chosen, and Andvari is a Dwarf. Dwarves are invaluable auxiliaries to the Æsir even though the poetic Edda does not insist on their importance. In order to illustrate this last statement, let us indulge yet another digression.

* * *

Digression 2 about the Dwarves' importance

Dwarves are the first ones to suffer from Ragnarök onset, as if they were the last barrier protecting the Æsir. This unclassical role attributed to them is given by stanzas 3 and 4 of Hrafnagaldur (see bibliography):

End of s. 3	End of s. 4
Þráinn's thought is	The doughtinesses with (of) the dwarves
a dream with a burden [a somnolence],	dwindle, the worlds
with dissimulation/conceit,	down to Ginnung
Dáinn's thought [is] a dream …	go down to sink.

* * *

It follows that all these characters are kind of special, important ones. It may then be appropriate to hypothesize that their örlög are in some ways different from the ones of commonplace persons.

Conclusion relative to Norns possible role at sending sköp

In the case of superhuman characters, we can thus conclude that the poets consider that örlög is similar to a gigantic and complex tangle of *sköp* each component of which is intertwined with all others, i.e. that örlög is similar to a system of *sköp*, each being symbiotic to all others. In a sense, this explains the hero's' way of speech when they avoid a shameful complaint about their örlög by blaming some Norns' sköp.

On örlög

Almost all the stanzas quoted here speak of örlög. This word is often inappropriately translated by 'destiny' or 'fate'. The weakness of this translation has already been explained in the above section dealing with the Norns. Similarly, the commonplace meaning of word 'destiny' in Lokasenna is rejected because, in this poem, örlög are declared as a knowledge including the future as well as the past. In Lokasenna s. 25, Frigg advises Loki not to speak about örlög because it exposes what he "*drýgðuð í árdaga* (perpetrated in old times)" and that it is better if "*firrisk forn rök firar* (the human ones avoid (to know) old rök [= 'past örlög'])."

It is useful here to point out the expression of Reginsmál stanza 14 where Reginn decides to adopt Sigurðr and to control him by an *örlögsími*, an örlög-string, a way of stating that he will dominate him by magic and will accordingly reshape his destiny. The full story showed us how Reginn lamentably failed to carry out this feat.

The taboo to use *sköp* for modifying örlög is also clearly expressed in § II-19, Fjölsvinnsmál 47: "*Urðar orði kveðr engi maðr, þótt þat sé við löst lagit* (with the word of Urðr no one finds fault, even if it is established by error)." All this confirms the conclusion of § II-14 by which we can consider örlög as a rough block upon which a magician-artist traces his *sköp* while carefully respecting the direction of the fibers composing the block.

Lastly, in § II-7, while commenting stanzas 1 and 3 of Völundarkviða, we already announced that the behavior of the three girls confirms the idea that örlög not only are binding us, but even more that we must *drýgja* (endure/ achieve/make) them without balking, possibly in suffering or in violence. Völundarkviða also teaches that örlög influence may look frozen for some time, and then it strikes humankind at a suitable moment. This 'suitable moment' is called '*munr*' in Old Norse and constitutes a possible root for the name of one of Óðinn's ravens, Muninn ('the' *munr*). A detailed explanation on the meanings of *munr* and its bonds with the unconscious is provided at 'Huginn and Muninn'. We will a little further see that *sköp* belong to the conscious of the wizard who handles them. On their side, örlög are clearly a magic that handles us without we being aware of it, until a *munr* takes place and 'a lightning opens our eyes'.

This is a way to state that örlög and sköp belong to our unconscious psyche, they differ in that örlög is an inborn unconscious characteristic of humankind's psyche, while *sköp* are 'born' outside, in a sorcerer mind. The *sköp* thus belong the conscious part of the wizard's psyche. This suggests that the 'sköp-ed' person may feel them as strangers inside him/her by which he/she becomes partly conscious as is someone who feels 'bewitched'. We will comment more this observation at the end of the next section on *sköp*.

On sköp

We could observe that '*sköp*' and their derivatives have many instances in Poetic Edda.

First of all, we should underline the considerable capacity shown by the *sköp* in shaping someone's life. This is clearly stated in Grípisspá, where Grípir accepts announcing his örlög to Sigurðr. As they are not very favorable, and since the last one is prone to anger, Grípir is anxious when he meets Sigurðr again. This last understands it and, to comfort Grípir, states (s. 53): *Skiljum heilir, mun-at sköpum vinna* ... (let us split happily, none can against *sköp* win ...). In Atlakviða, Guðrún attributes to the *sköp* (*sköpum viðr manngi*: against the *sköp*, nobody can anything) the fact that she did not succeed in warning her brothers of the treachery Atli planned for them.

Hávamál 84 is a special case in the sense that past participle *sköpuð* has been so often translated in a way that forgets its magic. It evokes women by saying that "*váru þeim hjörtu sköpuð* (their hearts were shaped)" on a revolving wheel, which many commentators read as implying that women are "fickle." Another more probable translation is the one of 'breaking', explained in Hávamál translation stanzas 6 and 84 (see s. 84 in § II-2.5). In turn, this can be understood as a statement that, in a civilization that does not respect femininity, it is true that their destiny is to be either breaking or broken, as Óðinn suggests. Unexpectedly, the recent women's revolts illustrate that women reject such shapings (may them be magic or not) from our civilization. But in the case of Hávamál quotation, we cannot neglect the possibility that the female hearts are thus "magically shaped" as if society would "throw *sköp* (fates) at them." In other words, we explain here that old Norse spirituality supports the claim that women's örlög (their inescapable fate) does not reflect all inborn features: much of what seems to be 'inborn' actually reflects the set of sköp 'thrown' at them by their social environment, as so often claimed by feminist speakers.

Hávamál 98 presents a negative version of *sköp* when Billingr's maid warns Óðinn that they both risk death if he does not yield to the necessary secrecy of their relationship because, in that case, "*allt eru ósköp* (we are both without *sköp*)." In this case, no-*sköp* takes obviously the meaning of 'no-future'. This way of speech is often used in the sagas to indicate a curse. Thus, we should not confuse unfavorable *sköp* as those unveiled by Óðinn about women and *ósköp* that announce imminent death. For example, in Reginsmál stanza 6, Loki utters a kind of curse addressed to Hreiðmarr: "*verðr-a sæla sköpuð* (not-will become happy (your) shaped)" where he modifies Hreiðmarr's *sköp*. This curse first effect appears quickly, and it will be carried on for years on his two sons. In the same way, in Sigurðarkviða in skamma stanza 7, Brynhildr complains that "*nornir skópu* (Norns shaped)" an unhappy life to her and Sigurðr, i.e. the cursing sköp have been carried on throughout their lives. This aspect of long duration feature is common to örlög and *sköp*.

We saw that, in the case of heroes, *sköp* and örlög merge more or less. On the other hand, when human beings feel the need to modify their örlög, they can try to build *sköp* that may be 'örlög-compatible', i.e. they do not oppose to the runes engraved by Norns.

Sköp design is almost always allotted to a human or divine sorcerer (Óðinn, Loki, Frigg) though exceptionally to Norns as it is explained in the above section "On Norns and their magic".

The fact that *sköp* are not automatically unfavorable is hinted at by Brynhildr who, in Sigurðarkviða in skamma stanza 58, says to Gunnarr that they could have been happy if "*góð sköp gerði verða* (good *sköp* had been granted to us)." This is confirmed by Gróa who, in Grógaldr 4, wishes her son to be protected from misfortune by Skuld's *sköp*. In a different way, in

Guðrúnarkviða in fyrsta stanza 24, Guðrún's sister states that Brynhildr brought "*illrar skepnur* (bad shapings)" in everyone's life: she needed to specify that they were unfavorable.

Earth creation is certainly not unfavorable and VafÞrúðnismál 21 teaches that it was shaped (*var jörð of sköpuð*) by Æsir who used Ymir's body.

It is necessary nevertheless to acknowledge that the number of complaints of misfortunes that the *sköp* could cause largely exceeds the good fortunes. To the ones already stated in this conclusion, we can add the following ones.

In Reginsmál stanza 2, dwarf Andvari complains to have been changed into a pike by the *sköp* of a Norn "*norn skóp* ... (a Norn shaped ...)".

In Oddrúnarkviða stanza 34, Oddrún confesses that she much complained of the *sköp* that herself and others shaped.

In Atlamál in grænlenzku, stanza 2, the warriors let grow the *sköp* that here seem to be the magic of a warlike fury.

In Atlakviða stanza 39, Guðrún, in the same way, "lets grow the *sköp* (*sköp lét hon vaxa*)" of her fury with the result of a gigantic slaughter.

In addition, Sigurðr is an excellent example of the difference between örlög and *sköp*. There no way Sigurðr would oppose his örlög. In Fáfnismál 11, however, he realizes that Reginn's magic will not be able to reach him, which he states as: "*verða-t svá rík **sköp*** (*sköp* [Reginn's] will thus lose their power)." He will hence be able to dominate Reginn's magic. Similarly, in stanza 44, the nuthatches predict his failure to awake Sigrdrífa, which will not happen because he will dare to slice her armor (and this action will cause to reinstall him inside his örlög). There again, Sigurðr's magic and daring are enough powerful to cancel the *sköp* announced by the nuthatches.

Here is a last example of how much *sköp* are compelling. A little before the slaughter described in Atlakviða, Högni, Guðrún's younger brother, and his wife must split and they share a last fatalistic glance: "*þá hygg ek sköp skiptu, skilðusk vegir þeira* (then I think the *sköp* had (them) appointed, their ways split)" because both know well that Högni was going to his death. Högni is a fierce warrior but this fierce warrior tenderly loves his wife and shares with her a last instant of love before Atli's warriors sköp and Gudrún's örlög send him in the middle of a slaughter.

The *sköp* are thus in general 'spells' or 'curses' thrown on a person by a wizard in order to modify the course of this person's life (in good or evil). In Reginsmál stanza 5 (§ II-11), the wizard, here Loki, has clearly in mind the reason why he throws this spell and he can explain it. All this suggests that Norse wizards were able to justify their *sköp*: They are not driven by their unconscious since they do not release their magic in an irresponsible way, randomly in the universe. This suggests that *sköp* belong to a class of conscious magic (to the wizard), whereas örlög belong to an unconscious (to everyone) magic.

The list of complaints about sköp given a few lines above bears witness to the possibility for sköp to become conscious in the mind of the 'sköp-ed' one. This observation leads us to think that they are a special kind of unconscious that would be qualified as "particularly energetic" in Jung's way of speech since they are always on the verge of reaching consciousness. In fact, they belong to a collective unconscious that would qualify as 'primitive thinking' by Jung, which explains that he does not feel the necessity to create a special category for them. We will, however see later, in § IV-1. 'Active introspection' archetype', that ancient ON psyche is far from being really primitive: this is why we feel necessary to include this archetype within the ones of humankind, no longer as a simple primitive artefact.

In turn, accepting the universalness of this special layer of our unconscious-conscious psyche, we may better interpret large amounts of the modern behaviors. In our society that mokes magic, most people quite cautiously avoid referring to magic behavior and replaced the ancient words by two equivalent words: propaganda and advertisement that share with sköp the feature to to be an unconscious on the fringe of becoming a conscious.

Sköp-born propaganda does not apply specifically to individual persons, it rather deals with crowds. A striking example of these refurbished sköp is given by the propaganda distributed on the worls-web. Each person may harmlessly express passionate hate or passionate love for a famous politician (say, for example President Trump) or a famous company (say for example, Montanso). Once the number of such advices heaps up to some extent, the classical change from individual to crowd creates a kind of attractive force to the heap. Each member of this crowd has been at the start unaware of his/her power, while later each of them becomes aware of their power. In other words, an unconscious power changed into a conscious one by the strength of their crowding. As the the crowd starts becoming huge it develops into a social being becoming increasibly dangerous to those who did not join this 'heap'. In terms of sköp, we can express this as follows: each individual opinion is nothing but a simple wish, though it becomes a string of sköp sent by a crowd of individuals.

We will only allude to the crude cheating performed by explicit so-called subliminal information that belongs a to an obvious way to twist reality by a direct action on our unconscious.

Sköp-born advertisement also directly act on our conscious, but they are harmless looking sentences hammered into each individual's conscious. Their point is not to generate a human crowd, but to generate inside each human mind a 'crowd' of redundant information that prevents each individual to freely think.

Both propaganda and advertisement aim to "make unconscious fools of us" but they use two different approaches, propaganda directly acts on our unconscious psyche in order to transform conscious individuals into members of a crowd of fools, advertisement directly acts on our conscious psyche by drowning each human mind in a crowd of similar messages, so as to decrease the conscious energy, thus enbling the unconscious one to take the leadship. Obviously, nothing prevents from using both techniques simultaneously.

The complexity of these two techniques playing with our conscious and unconscious sides does not ensure their originality. It might even be that they are simple subsets of the way Old Norse wizards have been playing their advertisement-propaganda games by sending elaborate sköp.

Sköp powers have been controlled in an ON civilization because it is impossible to modify örlög, after they have been stated by the Norns. Modern society ignores örlög as we have seen above, hence the destructive power of these modern sköp cannot be constrained and their power has already been noticed as very destructive more for the worse of our lives than for their best.

Curiously enough, it seems that Earth (known as Frigg in ON mythology) herself becomes also less and less tractable.

About rök

Let us at first recall famous Snorri Sturluson's confusion between *rök* and *rökr* (or *rökkr*). It seems that he quite simply preferred an allegorical meaning (twilight) to Fjölsvinnsmál s. 14 direct meaning: "*unz rjúfask Reginn* (until the gods break)". This difference is not even an error and it does not deserve its destructive celebrity.

This being said, it remains that the four uses of 'rök' in poetic Edda deserve discussion.

a – Rök as a part of örlög
- Hávamál stanza 145 says that Óðinn engraved the "*fyr rök …*" (before rök) which drove the future destiny of humankind.
- Lokasenna stanza 25 speaks about the gods' "*forn rök* (past rök)." Thus, not only örlög cover history of the present and history of the past, but there is a form, rök, which means 'a part of örlög'.

b – Rök as a redundant way to point at örlög

In the two other instances, the word rök is used in an emphatic and redundant way as being the 'entirety of particular parts'.
- VafÞrúðnismál stanza 42, "*tíva rök öll* (the entirety of the gods' rök)" i.e. all parts of the god's örlög.
- Alvíssmál stanza 9 says that Alvís knows "*öll rök* (all rök)", then identical to the whole örlög. These two forms are rendered by "all destiny" in the traditional translations which, do not render the symbiotic nature of the parts of "örlög" or "all sköp." A special case is the one of Alvíssmál, where Þórr addresses several times Alvís by "*vitir öll rök fíra* (you understand all humankind's rök)." Here, emphasis is obviously ironical, which agrees with the situation of a Dwarf coming to claim Þórr's daughter in marriage.

On mjötuðr

We met the word *mjötuðr* in several Eddaic poems. Namely, in Völuspá 2 (*miötviðr*) and 46 (*miötuðr*), in Oddrúnarkviða 14, Fjölsvinnsmál 18 and Sigurðarkviða in skamma 71. Our comment of this last stanza explains the possible interpretations of this word.

Mjötuðr is the 'measurer', who tells the measure of things, similarly to a worldwide orchestra conductor. According to the context, it will mean in Norse either (optimistic view) a god, a guard, or (pessimistic view) a plague. Thus, this word indicates an organizer who can be either favorable or unfavorable. The commentators were deeply influenced by a similar

Anglo-Saxon word: *meotud* or *metod* that means 'destiny, creator, God, Christ'. In this language, *metod* points only at the optimistic side of the measurer. The simultaneously negative aspect in ON *mjötuðr* is rendered, in Anglo-Saxon, by the close word *metodsceaft*: 'creation/construction of *metod*' which means 'decree of the destiny, doom, death'. The unconscious influence of *metod* shows up by a propensity to associate this word to the Christian God by forgetting the existence of *metodsceaft*. For example, CV, at *mjötuðr*, speaks of the existence of *meotud* (or *meotuð*) in Anglo-Saxon homilies with the meaning of God. On the other hand, when it gives the meaning 'plague' (*bane*), it forgets to announce the existence of *metodsceaft* which exactly means 'plague'. It follows that, even though Anglo-Saxon civilization identifies *meotud* and God, Norse civilization keeps the double meaning of *mjötuðr* and the meaning of 'destiny' stays the one of 'what gives the measure of our lives', not the one of God. This is confirmed by Oddrúnarkviða, stanza 16, § II-15, that compares Brynhildr's measure to the one the cosmic measurer, Yggdrasill.

On a similar trend, the occurrence in Völuspá s. 2: *miötvirð*, pointing at Yggdrasill, has been regarded as a scribal error by CV. First of all, it should be noticed that Völuspá quotes Yggdrasill tree very often: In stanza 2, it is called *miötvirðr*; in 27th: *helgi baðmr* (holiness-tree); in s. 46: *miötuðr*, when it starts to burn; in s. 47, Yggdrasill becomes *aldna tré* (ancient tree) and in s. 57th *aldrnara* (old nourisher)–when it is burning in full. Thus, in stanza 2, it is still the tree of the measure and, in the 27th, the crowned tree, because the flames did not reach it yet. In stanzas 46 and 47, when Ragnarök is set up, it starts to burn, it is named three times by pointing out its three functions (*mjötuðr, yggdrasill* and *ancient tree*). Lastly, in s. 57, when Ragnarök fully holds, it is not any more a tree but a burning stump, a thing of the past, a 'former nourisher'. Some people see here an allusion to the fact that fire is used to cook food: fire is not always destroying. During Ragnarök's accomplishment, however, Yggdrasill itself is destroyed (not cooked!) and this is why it has been necessary to remember in s. 2, 27, 46 that, until Ragnarök begins, Yggdrasill has still been a divine tree.

In our civilization, trees are things and to see them as being divine looks immensely primitive and ridiculous. In a surprising way, however, the trend of personalizing them, if not of divinizing them, became again significant under the influence of ecology and the realization that humankind is unable to avoid global warning, the spectacular decrease of biological diversity and a still discrete desertification.

CHAPTER III

How Much Reliable is the Poetic Edda?

In this chapter we will use five different sources.

One is devoted to Hávamál, and makes use of Evans (1986) commentaries. The second one is due to Carolyne Larrington (1993),—abbreviation: "StoreCS."

The third is devoted to Völuspá. It is "The Nordic Apocalypse" (2013)—abbreviation: "NordAp."

The fourth and fifth ones are translations of Hávamál and Völuspá (see bibliography).

III-1. A few general remarks

As a first *caveat* we have to clearly state that we do not deal here with Snorri's account of the Eddaic poems. His concern clearly is teaching the basic knowledge of ancient poetry to a new generation of poets who lost contact with this kind of knowledge. Anticipating somewhat on the conclusion of the present book, we can say that Snorri's prospect is quite different from the one of Poetic Edda publishers, i.e. providing, to the best of their own knowledge, the most faithful account of ancient poetry.

Let us, as second *caveat*, recall the profusion of texts which deal with the problem of humankind's destiny and the world end. This line of thought is called an "eschatology." There are therefore many eschatologies, Christian, Islamic, Jewish, Buddhist etc. each inspired by the worldview of the religion that produced it. The medieval success of some 'pagan' literature, named

Sibylline Oracles is presented by Wikipedia as follows: "in their existing form (they) are a chaotic medley ... The final arrangement, thought to be due to an unknown editor of the 6th century AD (Alexandre), does not determine identity of authorship, time, or religious belief; many of the books are merely arbitrary groupings of unrelated fragments." In such a messy medley, all kind of ideas, possibly contradictory ones, are freely gathered. It is then easy to find spurious resemblances between Völuspá and some parts of the *Sibylline Oracles* ... and to dub them 'Christian influences'.

Here is a simplified example of a particularly cumbersome argument:

1. **Ursula Dronke (1997, pp. 99–104) investigated the possibility of Christian influences due to similarities between Völuspá and the Sibylline Oracles that have been very popular during the Middle Ages.**
2. **Karl G. Johansson (NordAp, pp. 161–184) disputed some of her points and refined Dronke's analysis using the so-called Tiburtine Oracles.**
3. **Stephen J. Shoemaker (ref: http in bibliography), reports that many modifications to the known texts of Tiburtine Oracles are in progress.**

This looks like a deliberate or naïve attempt to muddy the waters.

Let us now share a third and last *caveat*, linked to the modern language rendering of the ON words used in the poetry. Here are two examples of this kind of this difficulty. As soon as we start reading Völuspá, its s. 1 uses the word *spjall* here translated as 'knowledge, learning' while its real meaning, at least in Völuspá, is closer to either an incantation or a saying. Another, more classical example is the one of '*siðr*' which we translate as 'religion'. In fact, '*siðr*' refers to a 'tradition' or a 'behavior' rather than to a religion: we could even say that the word 'religion' does not exist in ON. We nevertheless observe that the old 'religion' is called '*forn siðr*' (old tradition) and the Christian religion is called '*nýr siðr*'. Does *siðr* now means 'tradition' or 'religion'? Such a change in the meaning of the words cannot happen overnight: this exemplifies the fact that the dates of a country Christianization (where the Christian way of life is generally accepted) are established much later than those of its Conversion (where the basic speech is still a pagan one).

Our goal here is not to get lost in the meandering of Christian influences contention but to offer Hávamál and Völuspá beautiful stanzas to modern minds lacking of religious prejudices and willing to study ancient Norse spirituality. It does happen, fortunately, that some Christian explanations are partially justified and their refutation enables a better understanding of an Old Norse text that is often obscure and always allusive.

III-2. Hávamál is free of 'Christian influences'

Possible Christian influences on Hávamál have been actively sought during the 19th and 20th centuries. This trend has been smothered by two scholars.

One is David Evans (1986) where he shows that there might exist superficial similarities between some Hávamál sentences and Christian texts sentences, but they apply to context that are so different that is impossible to match their respective meanings. (By parenthesis: We will argue in a similar way in the case of Völuspá.)

The other one is Carolyne Larrington (1993), who refuted K. von See arguments relative to a possible influence on Hávamál of the *Disticha Catonis* from the 3rd or 4th century, a popular Latin textbook during the Middle Ages.[6]

In the first part of this chapter, we will summary or reshape their reasoning in order to be able to firmly state that Hávamál has the same testimony value than archeologic finds, that is, an archaeological jewel of Scandinavian paganism. Obviously, this does not preclude that it is always forged as an interpretation derived from the knowledge of the archaeologists, here the commentators.

In its second part, heartened by the first one, we will dare handling Völuspá in a 'paganocentric' view, as opposed to the large number of Christocentric views that became academic ones during the last two centuries.

---

[6] This study has been also carried by John McKinnel, in "Essays on Eddic Poetry," Univ. Toronto Press, 2014, pp. 3–33 and 59–152. His presentation complicates the topic to such extent that we could not include it in this book.

III-2.1. Evans' arguments

First of all, we must remember the first onslaught of Christian influences refuted by Evans led in particular by Hagman, Boyer and von See who, in a somewhat elementary way, relied on vocabulary similarities in sentences dealing with disputably common themes. This approach does not provide convincing results because the vocabulary may be similar, but the thematic similarities are still non-existent or superficial (or even ridiculous). Let us now illustrate the value of these three scholars' arguments. Evans general advice is as follows: the "view of the poem as purely native and heathen has, however, been challenged sporadically, especially in recent years, by claims that some of the strophes betray Biblical or Classical influences, or can be paralleled by and therefore perhaps derive from medieval proverbs in the Continental vernaculars."

Hagman

Nore Hagman claimed being able to provide many supposed similarities with 'Ecclesiasticus'. The following example, dubbed by Evans as "the closest of Hagman's parallels" enables us to appreciate the unconvincing power of this kind of claim.

(Ecclesiasticus 29. 22)	Hávamál 36
Better is the life of a poor man under a shelter of logs	The best is to own a place where to live even though it is small
than sumptuous fare in another man's house.	each man is (feels good) at home; although he only owns two goats and his dwelling is roofed by (mere) ropes, this is better, though, than (being compelled to) beg.

Both statements do evoke the superiority of humble life on a more prosperous one, a point so common in pre-Christian philosophy that it might be born from a general common sense. Note also that these two statements deeply differ because the gist of Ecclesiasticus is to oppose poverty to sumptuousness, while Hávamál opposes a humble way of life to begging (more or less equivalent to homelessness). Also significantly, Ecclesiasticus uses a plain way of speech, while Hávamál provides a poetic description of an easygoing simplicity rather than one of poverty as Ecclesiasticus does.

We could however believe that the two texts share 'general human commonsense' statements if many other such similarities were observed, which is negated by Evans.

Boyer-1

Régis Boyer claims also to have spotted striking resemblances with Proverbs and Ecclesiastes. Here again is one of these 'striking resemblances':

Proverbs 27. 17	Hávamál s. 57
Iron sharpeneth iron; so a man sharpeneth the countenance of his friend.	A brand from another brand burns, until burning out, flame self-kindle from flame; human being from human being becomes known when they meet in their speech a moody and isolated one, though, (becomes such) from his self-conceit.

Both do compare the behavior of two kinds of substances that influence the same substance and transfer the comparison to human behavior. There is indeed here a similarity at a very high level of generality. Note that iron does not communicate directly its 'sharpness' to another piece of iron while burning wood does. This Proverb evokes some confrontation between the two pieces of iron (thus between the two persons) while Hávamál points at speech bringing an agreement in the human-human interaction. Besides, this Proverb does not deal with a possible failure of the sharpening process, while the last line of s. 57 states that the 'speech process' may fail if one of the two partner shows self-conceit.

If Hávamál would evoke two warriors learning their skill then we could speak of a 'striking similarity' but it does evoke a peaceful relationship. Anyhow, at such a high level of generality and as noted by Evans: "the Book of Proverbs contains over eight hundred stanzas, practically all of them gnomic remarks based on observation and experience of life in a materially simple society," thus a total loss of similarity is highly improbable. In the particular case we just treated, we simply have shown their widely different contexts.

Boyer-2

Compares one short sentence of Proverbs with two stanzas in Hávamál:

Proverbs 25. 21	**Hávamál s. 3–4**
If thine enemy be hungry, give him bread to eat;	There is need of a fire for whom came in the house and has frozen knees. Meats and clothes are a man's need who traveled from the other side of the mountain.
and if he be thirsty, give him water to drink	Of water is need to whom for a meal comes, (for) a towel and a great reception

Again, strangely enough, Proverb statement is a recommendation for showing some kind of empathy for one's enemy, while Hávamál recommends having care of needing travelers in s. 3 and offering a hearty welcome to guests in s.4. Moreover, it systematically advises defiance for "non-friends" (hence for enemies). Seeing some 'Christian charity' for enemies in Hávamál is akin to misunderstanding its whole meaning.

Klaus von See

Introduces a concept he states as a Christian one and he calls it "uncertainty of earthly things" and he refers to Hávamál s. 81 as an instance of this concept. This stanza reads as:

In the evening will the day be praised,
a woman, who is burnt,
a sword, which is tried,
a maid, who is engaged,
ice, upon which walking is possible,
bier, which is drunk.

Evans disagrees with this comparison, and states that: "mutability becomes a Christian theme only when it is brought into contrast with the security and permanence of Heaven," and somewhat wickedly choses to comment on the last line of the stanza to say "It is going rather far to claim that a piece of advice like 'Don't praise ale until you have drunk it' implants the Christian moral of the transience and unreliability of this poor fleeting life!" Without recourse to irony, we can observe that s. 81 provides six examples, all of them are very earthly instances of some unreliability of earthly things. They do not pretend to any kind of spirituality that rests nowhere else than in von See's head.

III-2.2. *Larrington's arguments*

The second onslaught is much more subtle and difficult to explain. It has been driven by the same Klaus von See we have recently cited. It was based on arguments relating to a text 'similar' to Hávamál, namely Hugsvinnsmál, an Icelandic translation of a Latin text from the 3rd or 4th century, called *Disticha Catonis* (also known as Distiches of Cato). It is possible to compare these texts with the portion of Hávamál advices relative to managing a rightful life, that is to say Hávamál stanzas 1–95 and 112–137. It seems that, unfortunately, Larrington's work did not reach a large enough credit to counteract a still widespread doubt about Hávamál historical value, which is included in a general hostility into confidence in the historical value of ancient Norse poetry. As a matter of fact, this hostility takes its source the unavoidable fact that this poetry has been written between the 13th and the 14th century and the suspicion of 'Christian influences' looks like to be mere common sense. Let us now, with Larrington's help, wipe out these suspicions in the specific case of Hávamál.

III-2.2.1. First manuscript dating. Let us at first compare the dating of Hávamál, the oldest manuscript of which is dated 'around 1270', and von See's references, Cato's Distiches, are dated 3rd–4th centuries thus considerably earlier than Hávamál. On the contrary, the two oldest manuscripts of Hugsvinnsmál are dated between '1400 and 1500' thus later than Hávamál (source: The Skaldic Database).

Von See's argument is based on the (possible) proof that the reading of Hugsvinnsmál and Distiches inspired Hávamál publishers. Since the dating is not in favor of Hugsvinnsmál, he needs to use both the Distiches and Hugsvinnsmál to claim that they inspired Hávamál.

III-2.2.2. Superficial resemblances and deep differences. Among Larrington examples, we noticed that some of Hugsvinnsmál advice use a formulation similar to the one of Hávamál and, simultaneously, they seem at first sight to poorly translate the corresponding *Distich*. Analyzing their fundamental meaning, we could notice that they actually transfer an advice much nearer to the one of the corresponding distich than to the one of Hávamál.

Here is an example of such a fact where two lines of Hávamál and Hugsvinnsmál are identical: Hávamál s. 6, lines 1–3 reads:

Hávamál s. 6	**Translation**
At hyggjandi sinni	Of his intelligence (*or* caution)
skyli-t maðr hræsinn vera	a human should not boast,
heldur gætinn at geði;	he/she should rather stay heedful in spirit;

Hugsvinnsmál s. 72	
Af hyggjandi sinni	Of his intelligence (or caution)
skyldi maðr óhræsinn vera	a human should be non-boastful
nema geraz þarfir þess;	unless a need arises;

The first two lines of Hávamál and Hugsvinnsmál are indeed almost identical. We shall now compare them to Cato's corresponding distich, II-18, which states:

Insipiens esto, cum tempus postulate aut res;	Be foolish, when the occasion demands it,
Stultitiam simulare loco prudentia summa est.	pretending stupidity may be the most prudent attitude.

It is quite obvious that this distich advises to hide one's thoughts (by pretending stupidity) if this is useful to the reader. We also can observe that this conclusion perfectly matches the one of Hugsvinnsmál ("unless need arises") and mismatches the one of Hávamál ("keep close attention to your mind"). Hugsvinnsmál and Cato's distich advise to fake giving up your thought if convenient, while Hávamál advises to carefully stay attached to one's thought, even if this is a disturbing one.

If we put these advices in the context of what is taught to children, a Christian child is advised to hide his/her disagreement to what she/he is taught while a Norse one is advised to keep in mind his/her own opinion. This small example illustrates how deeply the two civilizations differ from each other. As a side-remark, note that the 13–14 century scholars who preserved their beautiful poetry from Christian influences seem to have followed Hávamál s. 6 counsel: "rather stay heedful in spirit" than Distich II-18 one of "pretending stupidity may be the most prudent attitude."

It follows that, even when Hávamál and Hugsvinnsmál share a few words, their intent widely differ from each other, which means that these common words do not express any commonality of thought. Otherwise stated, who 'influenced' whom is nonsensical.

We will now come back to Larrington's proper arguments that will, again and again, prove the weakness of von See's arguments.

III-2.2.3. Hávamál is 'unsophisticated'.

Commentators to Hávamál have often expressed the opinion that, especially its stanzas 1–95, provide a quite down-to-earth advising. This vague feeling cannot be properly used as an argument proving it is older than Hugsvinnsmál. Larrington has been able to provide a specific argument showing that Hávamál may, on some common topics, be less sophisticated than Hugsvinnsmál.

Her argument makes use of the existence of a stylistic form used by Norse poems, which consists in starting a sentence with a pair of adjectives linked by an '*ok*' (and), in the purpose of challenging the reader and drawing his/her attention on the person these adjectives qualify. Hugsvinnsmál presents three instances of such an arrangement:

"*Ráðhollr ok réttdæmr*" ('giving good advice you can trust' and 'well-adjusted example').
"*Þarflátr ok þakklátr*" (humble and grateful)
"*Slægr ok langþögull*" (cunning and long-silent).

Note that these pairs of adjectives define a subtle qualification since the second adjective specifies and intensifies the state of the person described. It is possible that a well-adjusted advice is not a good one, to be grateful without humility and being long silent without being cunning. The two similar pairs in Hávamál carry a more naïve way of speech:

"*Þagalt ok hugalt*" (silent and attentive)
"*Þveginn ok mettr*" (washed and satiated).

We can hardly be attentive without being silent and 'washed and satiated' alludes to a down-to-earth situation.

In this sense, the pagan way of speech is more obvious, less subtle than the Christian one. Hugsvinnsmál more sophisticated way of speech supports a later dating than Hávamál.

III-2.2.4. Arguments relative to the worldviews implied by these three texts.
Some of von See's arguments use a statement that the texts use metaphors reflecting a particular worldview common to all three. Here is a detailed example.

Von See asserts that Hávamál stanza 79 and Hugsvinnsmál 74 are both derived from Cato's distich II-19 that states (in Latin):

Run away from lust (*luxuria*),
and avoid as well the crime of avarice;
both destroy a good repute (*fama*).

Hugsvinnsmál 74 reads as:

From guilty avarice
you should go away,
love of flesh is hateful;
higher fame ('*orðstír*')
never a man will reach
than to guard against sin.

Both refer to avarice and sexual pleasure as a way to ruin a good repute. In other words, Hugsvinnsmál is here a faithful translation of Cato's distiches and both carry the same worldview: avoiding sins is the best way to keep a good repute.

Let us now see what says Hávamál stanza 79, of which von See claims it bears the same world view:

> A non-wise person
> if he happens to acquire
> wealth or the pleasure of a woman
> (his) pride (*metnaðr*) (over-) waxes
> but never does (his) good sense:
> he plentifully proceeds in (self-) conceit.

This stanza speaks of wealth that is not automatically greed, and probably refers to the sexual pleasure of a man who has access to "female pleasure," (which is ambiguous as who receives pleasure). Distich II-19 teaches that "greed and sex" prevent from a good repute, while Hávamál teaches that pride in wealth and sex prevent from good sense and drives to conceit.

This means that Distich II-19 states that abstinence drives to social respect, while Hávamál indicates that the pride in sex and earning the pleasure of a woman 'guards against' good sense and causes conceit. This is deeply different from Hugsvinnsmál Distich II-19 teaching that "greed and sex" prevent from a good repute, because Hávamál says that pride is the cause of bad repute, instead of greed and sex. Besides, in Hávamál, the deep cause of conceit is the lack of wisdom (asserted in the first line) which makes lack of wisdom as being the primary 'sin' of Old Norse worldview.

We are then entitled to conclude that, even if the wording of this stanza of Hávamál could have received some inspiration from the Distiches, it carries a pagan worldview, obviously very much prior to Christianization since lack of wisdom is 'devilish' instead of sexual practice.

We nevertheless should observe, from their example, that flipping through the Distiches or Hugsvinnsmál may suggest superficial commonalities to Hávamál. Their common feature is that the three deal with how leading an honorable life in the society to which their author belongs. We have just noted on the example chosen by von See that Distiches refer to a Christianized Latin society, Hugsvinnsmál to a Christianized Norse society and Hávamál to a pagan society, as one would have expected.

III-2.2.5. Conclusion. We already discarded the 'first onslaught' in § III-2.1. Now that the second and last onslaught is also discarded, we have carefully answered to the suspicion of Christian influences that the academic community could reasonably suggest. We are thus free to claim that Hávamál is a trace of a genuine pre-Christian Norse thought.

It is indeed still bewildering—nowadays—that a poem preserved by purely oral knowledge until the year 1270, has not undergone significant modifications. Moreover, we know that the authorization to practice the ancient religion in Iceland in private was canceled around 1020, and thus Hávamál was outlawed during these 250 years of intense Christianization. How have Icelanders been able to keep a faithful memory of these 164 stanzas? A way to decrease our surprise is to note that such a memorization is far from being impossible. For example, it is certain that the custom of the recitation of the laws (oral, with prohibition to use 'notes') by the Thing 'Speaker' has just been kept pretty much until that time. There then existed at least one group of Icelanders who had the capacity to memorize texts longer and more boring than Hávamál and even the few thousand stanzas of Edda prestigious poetry, often 'built' on purpose to promote memorization.

The only possible explanation for this is that a 'faction' of scholars refused to let go this ancient poetry they loved so much and which recalled old stories of past pride. An obvious example of such a behavior has been provided by Snorri Sturluson who promoted and secured some 50 year before them a large amount of this kind of knowledge. These people have protected Hávamál from any Christian influence, at least from what would have been incongruous in the context of the old religion. It may not have been kept exactly "identical" (identical to what?—it is not impossible that there were several different versions already during pagan times), but at least so that it relates what these learned men still knew of the ancient customs in the middle of the 13th century. They would then provide a text carefully expurgated of any Christian influence.

This statement may look farfetched if we did not have the example of the Icelandic rune poem that does not refer to God, as anyone can easily check: As nicely stated by Caroline Larrington (1993, p. 134) when speaking of the Old English rune poem, she states: "Unlike the studiously unchristian Icelandic version, the [Old English] Rune Poem frequently refers to God."

When analyzing the texts of people who really argued deeper than a simple "it is obvious" in favor of Christian influences, we can be very surprised at their naiveness. It is even possible that the redactors of the Eddaic poems, wanting to deceive their Christian censors, willingly introduced some words evoking Christianity, sprinkling them in places where the context supports a pagan understanding instead of a Christian one. This assertion might seem too gross to be true, though it naturally comes to the mind after thinking over a few of these 'influences'.

III-3. Christian influences on Völuspá?

It is simply impossible to reply in this book to all the existing arguments claiming the presence of 'Christian influences' in Völuspá since they not only swarm about, but they often are not consistent among them. A more detailed presentation of them is found in nordic-lifeVolu : it is as complete as possible while avoiding boring repetitions and it presents 19 arguments (and one hypothesis) against this kind of influences legitimacy, answering to the 19 available reasonable arguments in favor of it.

III-3.1. Völuspá s. 1

Stanza 1 translation reads:

Line 1:   I beg you to listen,
          you all of the family,
          higher and lower ones,
          children of Heimdalr;
L. 5:   You want, Valföðr, that
          I properly tell
          ancient knowledge
          remotest that I remember.

In the first verse, "begging to listen" instead of imposing silence to the audience illustrates a typical Norse behavior which, with all due respect to the poet or the völva, indicates a kind of humility seldom met among religious preachers.

The word 'knowledge' in L. 7 partially render the ON word *spjall* that does mean 'knowledge, a maxim' but it also carries the meaning of 'magic incantation'. In other words, what we call 'knowledge of the past' is also, at least partly, a tale of magic which implies that magic is always associated to knowledge, a fact that totally disappeared from the structure of our way of thinking. In a sense, no part of Völuspá lacks an implicit constant reference to magic: 'understanding' it carries a kind of implicit lie if magic is not explicitly recalled when commenting this poem. Again, in our civilization, it became impossible to render magic without using a conceited speech that we shall avoid in the following.

The rational reader, nevertheless should not forget that throughout the poem, he/she sails on waters he/she believes to be murky, and this helps him/her to avoid blindly thrusting a Christian context of Völuspá into a pagan one.

III-3.2. *Völuspá s. 2*

> I remember the Giants
> in old times born,
> those who in the past
> nourished me to become an adult;
> I remember nine countries,
> nine Giantesses
> and the famous measure-master
> still under the ground.

In this second stanza, the völva describes the oldest times she had known: the universe amounts to nine distinct worlds inhabited by "Giants and Giantesses" able to raise their children. Since "the famous measure-master," that is to say Yggdrasill, is still growing under the ground, this suggests that gods and humans do not exist yet, and that the völva has grown is this primary world, probably as being herself a Giantess.

The last two lines introduce us to a 'being' that is so absent from our consciousness that we tend to somewhat forget the existence of an ancient tree who gives the good measure to our lives. He/She/It was 'still under the earth' as stated by line 8 of this stanza, implying that, during these remote times, the 'good measure' was not yet available. This means that these ancient times were times of wild immoderation.

We cannot avoid noticing here the huge difference, relative to the organization of the living beings, between the Christian tradition and the Norse one. In the Norse tradition, the first inhabitants were Giants and, equally important in the poem, Giantesses. This overall equality between males and females opposes the biblical description of the first earth inhabitants. The same occurs here for humankind: As already underlined in § II-1.1 (Humankind and its destiny) men and women have been both simultaneously gifted with the same abilities by the Powers, which again opposes the biblical legend of humankind's creation.

III-3.3. *Völuspá s. 4*

> At first Burr's sons,
> raised and exalted the grounds,
> where Miðgarðr stands,
> magnificently "*scópo*" (magic-shaped);
> The sun was shining from the South
> on a hall of stone,
> then were growing on the ground
> green leeks.

Let us first underline three interesting information.

One is that the gods (Burr's sons) "exalted the grounds" which carries the idea that they have been sanctifying Earth. It is quite amusing to note how much the presently raising move towards ecology pushes so many people to claim that the whole of our Earth is sanctified ground (as this stanza implies) as opposed to special locations that have been sanctified by the Churches.

The second is that, as soon as the Sun starts shining, then the first 'majestic herb' is humble leek, which nowadays is looked upon as a 'second rate' vegetable, except perhaps in Wales where it is still part of the national emblem. Völuspá pushes it towards the top of Pagan Northern faith—a remarkably forgotten truth, even among Heathens.

The third is relative to 'magic-shaped Miðgarðr'. Miðgarðr' is humankind's dwelling and the ON word for 'magic-shaped' is *scópo*. It is a 'strong form' of the preterit of verb *skapa* meaning 'to shape' and is very often simply rendered by 'to do'. As explained in the General Introduction of this book and illustrated in Chapter II, the plural of the associated substantive *sköp* carries the meaning of 'fate, magic spell'. In the particular case of s. 4, and in a context that accepts the existence of magic, we cannot understand how Earth could have been shaped without ancient Norse people linking it to magic.

The main argument associated to this stanza has been raised by Ursula Dronke (1997, pp. 115, 116) where she detects a striking influence of Genesis 1–9 on Völuspá s. 4. We shall now explain why her arguments amount to choose how Earth has been created: Was it process similar to 'giving birth' or one similar to 'putting things back in order'?

Since Burr's sons "raised the land," it has been raised from somewhere. If we refer to classical Norse mythology, it is reasonable to believe that it has been raised out of the primary huge hole, Ginnungagap. Dronke suggests another mechanism, by which it could have been raised out of the water (and we may accept that Ginnungagap depth might be full of water). Another argument in favor of Dronke's hypothesis is provided by Völuspá s. 59 that states: "*upp koma ... iörð ór ægi* (upward is coming ... the land out of the ocean)." Based on this hypothesis, Ursula Dronke says she has looked for another example of such an Earth emergence from the waters and she modestly confesses that the only allusion she could find of such a phenomenon is found in Genesis 1, 9. Let us now recall these verses: Genesis 9 and 10 state:

(9) And God said, Let the waters under the heavens be gathered up in one place, and the dryness appear. And that was.

(10) God called the dry land Earth, and the waters that were gathered together he called Seas. And God saw that it was good.

It seems quite clear that genesis does not describe an emergence of Earth out of the waters but a split-up between waters and land where 'God' piles up waters in one place and calls 'Earth' what remains, while Burr's sons have raised earth (earth is the moved part) to the effect it appears in (or out of) Ginnungagap. In both cases, Earth comes in existence, but it results from two different actions, one is to move away the waters, the other to expose Earth. The image evoked by the Norse myth is the one of maternal waters giving birth to the earth. Genesis 9 and 10 evoke a change of organization since 'God' takes the waters apart from the earth.

As it often happens, Christian and Heathen miracles superficially look similar, while their intimate mechanisms are widely different. In the Old Norse view, 'Earth' is goddess Frigg and the ON myth attributes to waters a creative power that indeed is not unique, as for example Aphrodite 'raising from the sea' (anadyomene) and Heimdallr 'born of nine waves'. In this case, Völuspá may tell that Frigg herself or a 'new goddess Frigg' are joining Gimlé.

The theme of an earth born of the waters as in Völuspá s. 4 (*Áðr Burs synir*) and explicitly in s. 59 (*sér hon upp koma*) may be also be commented from a non-religious point of view: the now large understanding on the way our own starting modern 'apocalypse' is going to take place.

Earth global heating is in itself a doom associated to sun fire and one of its consequences, the rise of ocean waters. In a sense we are facing an extinction of humankind due two factors. One is the fire as announced by Ragnarök as told by Völuspá. The other is a 'remake' of the six thousand years old Flood as described in Sumerian mythology around 4000 BCE and reused in numerous more recent mythologies.

All this brings us very far from any possible Christian influence.

III-3.4. *Völuspá s. 4 to s. 38*

Quite often, superficial arguments in favor of a 'striking similarity' between Völuspá and Medieval world-vision are pushed forward with very small convincing strength.

For example, let us consider the first four lines of s. 38, beginning with "*Sal sá hon standa…*"

> I see a <u>hall</u> standing (*Sal sá hon standa…*)
> far from the sun
> in Náströnd,
> all its doors face North…

Véstein Ólason (NordAp, pp. 25–44) claims the content of this stanza "could easily have been added to the poem in the twelfth or even thirteenth century." This kind of claim is obviously possible though totally unconvincing for two concordant reasons.

1. Archeological results tend to suggest that these halls are remains of an ancient tradition within the Scandinavian world as reported by many archeologists. For instance, Marianne Hem Eriksen (see bibliography) notes increasingly large halls since the fifth century and Anna S. Beck (see bibliography) informs her readers that: "In all, information of 270 longhouses from 85 sites (41 on Sealand, 44 in Scania) was collected."

2. The word used here to point at a hall is not *höll* but *salr*. In her paper in Viking Worlds (2015) Lydia Carstens argues about a difference of timing in the use of these two words. In order to claim that, for one, *salr* is much older than *höll* because the first is used mainly in poetry, while the second appears mostly in prose. For two, she uses a slight difference in their meanings: *höll* appears to apply only to a kingly hall, while *salr* cannot. Kings appearing late in Scandinavia, *salr* is the oldest of the two words.

Independently of the *salr*/*höll* debate we have also to take into account that this stanza specifies the doors of this *salr* have been opening to the North. Relying again on archeology, we know that longhouses dated 720–970 generally offer two entrances, one on each side of the longer portion of the house, but they are not 'facing each other', as it has been traditional since Bronze age (i.e. from 13th BCE) until 720 (Eriksen 2019 pp. 44). That the *salr* in s. 38 opens only to the North underlines its use for welcoming creatures of the North. Since Surtr comes from the South, this feature implies that Yggdrasill is attacked from the two main sides, North and South.

III-3.5. *Völuspá s. 39 (since this stanza numbering varies depending on the publisher, note that it starts with: Sá hon þar vaða...)*

A paper due to Henning Kure (NordAp, pp. 79–91) compares Revelation 21.8 and Völuspá s. 39.

Revelation 21.8 reads as:

"But the fearful, and unbelieving, and the abominable, and murderers, and fornicators (H. Kure version; in the Bible society version: whoremongers), and sorcerers, and idolaters, and all liars, shall have their part in the lake which burns with fire and brimstone: which is the second death."

Kure's modification to the 'official' version is significant since, as a knowledgeable expert, he is aware that prostitution and 'whores' have not been often spoken of in the sagas. Female slaves were enough and no particular shame (as opposed to Christendom) was associated to deal or to have sex with them. Let us at once throw away the possible allusion to whoremongers in Völuspá.

The six first lines of Völuspá s. 39 are as follows:

39. *Sá hon þar vaða*	Sees she there to wade
þunga strauma	(in) heavy streams
menn meinsvara	people perjurer ones
oc morðvarga,	and criminal-monsters,
oc þannz annars glepr	and who of others wheedles (or misleads)
eyrarúno;	ear-secret wives;

Both texts point out some people who clearly misbehaved in some way. Punishing sinners indeed is very typical of a Christian context, though we should not forget that the Old Norse civilization had its own definitions of criminality.

A 'wading' parenthesis

Let us at first note that Norse criminals "wade in heavy streams", which is quite different from "having a second death in a lake burning with fire" or having one's "part in the lake." We know of several cases where some Norse figures have been so wading without evoking any social degradation.

The most famous case is the one of god Þórr and his companion Þialfi. *Þórsdrápa* (Praise of Þórr) s. 8 tells us that during their travel to Giantland they "*flaut* (floated—usually translated by 'waded' when describing people) in the turf-flowing bog (the ocean)." Similarly, *Hervarar saga ok Heiðreks* describes how Hervör waded to find her father's barrow and ask him his magical sword. In both cases, the living waders are highly praised: they cannot be compared to any Christian sinners.

It follows that the content common to the two descriptions reduces to "criminal people will be singled out and move in a very unpleasant environment," which becomes much less striking than it was at first sight.

Kure is certainly far from ignoring that such a 'wading' is evoked in another poem, Reginsmál, s. 4 where Loki asks Andvari what price slanderers pay for having wounded other men. Andvari answers that "they must wade through Vaðgelmir..." which evokes a punishment. On the contrary, Grímnismál s. 21 tells that the dead warriors moving towards Valhöll have to cross a river whose "current seems too mighty for the *valglaumi at vaða* (*valr-glaumr* = dead warrior-cheer) to wade (it)." It thus describes a happy gang of heroes on their way to Valhöll. From these examples, Kure (p. 86) suggests that since "there is no similarity to Revelation involved in this case, which may indicate the wading to be an original Nordic trait."

We are thus left wondering what has been Kure's intention in comparing Revelation 21.8 and Völuspá s. 39.

Völuspá speaks of people who indeed violated three of the main Norse rules of honor, namely a "criminal-monster" who killed someone and did not claimed it (so preventing his family to start wergild negotiations), an 'oath perjurer' that describes a particular liar not identical to "all liars" stigmatized in Revelation, and a "seducer of confidante" who thus steals from this woman information precious to her official companion. We have no striking instance of this last crime in which sex is secondary as compared to the implied secret information loss. On the contrary, two famous oath perjurers are well known. Hávamál s. 110 declares, as a comment of his Gunnlöd's forsaking:

> Oath on the ring Óðinn,
> think I, had granted;
> what is to believe of his sincerities?

These lines tell that Óðinn himself perjured his oath to Gunnlöð—a capital Norse shame. That he indeed simultaneously lied to her is of little import in this myth.

The other instance his Sigurðr's and Brynhildr's oaths evoked in Sigrdrífumál s. 31:

"*It munuð alla*	You two together will want all
eiða vinna	oaths work out
fullfastliga,	fully-firm ones
fá munuð halda.	few will you be able to keep."

We know that Sigurðr will drink a magic potion concocted by Grímhildr that will make him forget his oath: that he had been drugged for it does not erase his shame for oath perjuring.

Again and again, there might be some similarities in the wordings used in Revelation 21.8 and Völuspá s. 39 while a deeper analysis of the context of these words shows how much widely they are different from each other.

III-3.6. s. 65 (Þá kømr inn ríki...) and s. 64 and 66

Let us end this list of refutations by analyzing s. 65, of which we know that it does not appear in Codex Regius (c. 1270) and is given by Hauksbók (c. 1307). Since these two dates go from times of free Iceland to the ones of a Norway protectorate (c. 1282), it is quite possible that some Norwegian clergy controlled Hauksbók edition of Völuspá and compelled the redactors to produce a somewhat 'Christianized' version.

Here is a literal translation of this stanza and its ON version:

Then arrives him powerful	*Þá kømr inn ríki*
at the gods' judgment,	*at regindómi,*
magnificent, coming down,	*öflugr, ofan,*
who on all advises.	*sá er öllo ræðr.*

The word *dómr* does mean 'judgement' but it can also mean 'state, condition' which, in this context, could also alludes to Ragnarök. We can thus understand this stanza as stating that, now that Ragnarök or Regindómr took place, 'someone' powerful comes from above and he will advise everyone on everything. The ancient gods had also been able to fly, then '*inn ríki*' could be either one of the surviving Æsir or a new still unknown god. This does not at all exclude Christ, though symmetrically it does not specially point at him.

The flabbiness of s. 65 is enhanced by the accuracy of s. 64 and the obvious paganism of s. 66.

Here is s. 64:

A <u>hall</u> sees she rising,
<u>shinier than the sun</u>
with gold as a roof
on <u>Gimlé</u>;
To this place the <u>faithful</u> ones go
people to settle
and for always
<u>of delight to benefit</u>.

A "hall shiner than the sun" may evoke oriental churches while, as far as we know, Scandinavian churches have not been gold covered. Pagan as well as Christian imagination may be both here at work.

Gimlé is the name of the new world that has been born from the waters, as stated by s. 59 (recalled in III-3.3, dealing with s. 4).

Again, the 'faithful ones' may be faithful to new Christianity or to *Forn Siðr*, the ancient (pagan) way of life. Similarly, "to benefit of an eternal delight" might be alluding to Christian paradise as well as to pagan Valhöll.

Stanza 64 is thus similar to s. 65 in that it is overall ambiguous in keeping open to the Christian faith. Both seem to describe the feelings of Christian people still 'polluted' with Heathen faith or, conversely, in the feelings of Heathen people doubtful of the Christian faith ability to bring a spirituality worth of their values.

It follows that s. 64 and 65 indeed provide a shaking approval of Christian values being forced upon half convinced Heathen ones. We could indeed qualify this as some 'rickety Christian influences'.

On the contrary, the last 66th stanza clearly alludes to the *forn siðr*. It says:

s. 66:
L 1. Here comes the dim one
dragon flying,
snake glimmering, up from below
from Waning-Moon Cliff (*Niðafjöll*);

it carries in its wings,—
it flies the meadow above—,
Níðhöggr (Insult-Stroke), corpses.
Now must she sink.

Since Yggdrasill has been burned, it looks quite logical that the dragon who lived in Yggdrasill's roots may have survived Ragnarök and be now free of flying in Gimlé sky. That it carries corpses in its wings simply means that life and death are still the two main humankind features, here heathen-way expressed by an allusion to a Giant who carries away crowds of dead bodies. This essential feature has been already expressed in Haustlöng by Þjóðólfr úr Hvíni (~855–930): Giant Þjazi (Iðunn's abductor) is evoked through the kenning "*margspakr már báru val-kastar*" (very-wise seagull of the wave of the 'caught' by death) in stanza 3 and by "*hrun-sæva hræva*" (beachcomber of the corpses) in stanza 11. These two kennings qualify Þjazi as a corpse carrier as Níðhöggr is here in lines 5 and 7.

> **That Þjóðólfr's famous poem might have influenced**
> **the redactors of Völuspá is infinitely more probable**
> **than any other external influence.**

III-3.7. *A deep poetical coherence within Völuspá*

Somewhat aside from the general trend of chapter III, it is interesting to notice a quieter approach to the poem, such as Gunnell's. In his contribution to (NordAp, pp. 63–77), Terry Gunnell avoids the theme of the influences in order to insist on the importance of considering aspects other than a textual one, such as its performance, thus including the voices, music and possible impersonations.

He notes that Völuspá s. 3, "almost lacking in hard consonants … stresses sonorant vowels, nasals (*m* and *n*), and echoed *s*, *v*, and *f* fricatives … all of which also serves to raise the final image …" of *Ginnungagap* from the rest of the stanza. Here is a subset of Gunnell's stressed syllables:

Ár var alda,
þar er Ýmir bygði,
vara sandr né sær

né svalar unnir,
iörð fannz æva
né upphiminn,
***g**ap var **g**innunga*
*enn **g**ras hver**g**i.*

Gunnell then comments: "The same open peaceful sounds accompany the times of natural 'creation' … and the reappearance of the new world from below the waves … after ragnarök" in Völuspá s. 59.

Sér hon upp koma
öðro sinni
iörð ór ægi
iðiagræna;
falla fossar,
flýgr örn yfir,
sá er á fialli
***f**isca **v**eiðir.*

Instead of stressing the differences between s. 3 Heathen earth and s. 59 'Christian' earth, Gunnell stresses their common features in the sounds they carry when they are spoken instead of being read. These remarks illustrate an approach where the whole poetic content of the poem is taken into account. It follows that it is no longer split into independent slices that destroy its poetic value. Such a destructive effect is perhaps the real, though at best unconscious, goal of all the seekers for Christian influences.

III-3.8. *Singing Völuspá*

In 1999 a musical group named Sequentia produced a CD in which they sing, in ON, several poems of the Edda. This work is cited as an example by Gunnell in (NordAp, pp. 63–77). Here is an example of their work for Völuspá s. 1, as it is given in a booklet joined to the CD:

1. *Hlióðs bið ek*
helgar kindir
meiri ok minni,

mögo Heimdallar;
Vildo at ek, Valföðr,
vel fyr telia
forn spiöl fíra,
þau er fremst um man.

Here is how this stanza is sung:
http://www.nordic-life.org/MNG/SequenciaEdda1999Volu1st.mp3
The beginning 'Hlióðs' and the long-lasting ending 'man' are easy to
spot. Now, the listener can better realize why this book tends to suggest that
the 'Christian influences' are in the modern minds of the readers or of the
musicians who sing Völuspá as a Christian church song. There have been
recent attempts at singing ON texts in a beautifully pagan way. For instance,
the group 'Skáld' (Le chant des Vikings 2019) provides a quite more 'viking-
like' version of several Edda poems.

In (NordAp, pp. 63–77), Terry Gunnell exposes a pronunciation well
adapted to the musical content of some stanzas of Völuspá. It seems probable that, in the original performances, the 'song' of the poem has been most
often limited to a recitative joined to a play on the various ways to utter the
ON language. Unfortunately, the language tricks providing these recitative
songs are mostly unknown, though Gunnell reveals a few of them.

III-4. Conclusion

It seems that some of 13th century scholars, who loved their literary past and
the beautiful Norse poems have not yielded to the power of Catholic thought.
On the contrary, some Norwegian and Icelandic scholars, as they also knew
Christian literature, were able to thoroughly expel any Christian allusion,
except for a few sentences absolutely necessary to satisfy the Christian censors, from the poems they had learned by heart before they were written.
In sum, they were able to minimize the influence of the churches as much
as possible. It seems that the first onslaught of the Christian influence theory has been now discarded regarding Hávamál. Inversely, these influences
are unduly still flourishing upon Völuspá. What we have just said in the
above section directly opposes the prejudices of modern commentators
who, strangely, have not made much of the work of Mrs. Larrington, now
25 years old.

Four Archetypal Images Carried by Hávamál and Völuspá

The purpose of this last chapter is very different from the one of Chapter III. We no longer try to show how much superficial are the arguments in favor of Christian influences but we conversely try to discover some hidden features included in the Poetic Edda. When we compare information relative to ON civilization to our own modern European one, we directly use the information provided by the ON text, as it stands, be it 'influenced' or not by any other civilization. We, however, by underlining in § IV-5.4 the difference in behavior between a pagan Óðinn and a Christian Anglo-Saxon king facing the same dilemma, will again reveal the huge difference between a pagan Norse worldview and a Christian one.

Since we shall deal with archetypes, we have to be very cautious in avoiding to confuse an archetype with its various images. For instance, speaking of religion and for the sake of avoiding confusion, let us denote by 'Religion' (with a capital R) a hypothetical archetype supposed to provide the structure of the images generated by the various pagan Norse religions and a Middle Ages Christian religion. This will drive us to analyze various archetypal images carried by Hávamál and Völuspá.

There exists another mistake to avoid when speaking of 'Norse religion' or of 'Norse unconscious images of their Religion archetype' as if they had been common to all Scandinavian people. Recent progress in archeology have proved how much 'local' and diverse could be Norse spirituality.

For instance, Norwegian archaeologist Sæbjørg Walaker Norddeide has worked on thousands of tombs in southern Norway and she has studied in detail a few hundred, the best-preserved ones, situated in nineteen sites, towns or villages. Instead of doing only 'averages' across the whole region, she presents tables of grave goods found in each chosen site according to their possible dating. Though each individual dating might be disputed, she deals with this uncertainty by presenting her observations as number of items certainly dated within a given period. Her curiosity and interest in each locality allowed her to note impressive variations, depending on the locality, in the way Christianization occurred in Norway.

We will start with an archetype carried by Hávamál by its s. 17 and s. 138. Several of these stanzas contain an allusion or even a straightforward description of an introspective behavior that seems to have been hardly noticed by most commentators. One possible cause to this fact may lie in the fact we tend to consider 'our' introspection as a rather passive mental attitude (sometimes even looked at as a kind of self-centered laziness) by which we observe our own thinking. The 'Old Norse introspection' described by Hávamál carries energy with it and is closely related to the actions of the introspective character. We thus will analyze the differences between our 'passive introspection' as compared to 'active introspection' as (poetically) suggested by several Hávamál stanzas.

In order to refute at once a possible criticism relative to the 'lack of new data' of our approach, let us make clear that we gather new information from something that seems to have been mostly neglected by the commentators: Instead of limiting our care to each isolated Hávamál stanza, we systematically looked for the relationships among stanzas, some being quite far from the others in the poem. This way of looking at Hávamál as a coherent poem instead of a sequence of disconnected stanzas often brings unexpected information upon which we have been basing our argumentation.

It will happen that, in order to achieve the first section conclusion, we needed to have a glimpse into another archetype, the one of 'death and life'. This second section will be as short as possible and will not treat of 'death and life' more than it has been necessary in order to complete section one: a more thorough presentation deserved by this topic needs at least one heavy book…

The third section focusses on Völuspá and contains an analysis of the Ragnarök theme itself.

A fourth one treats of the difference and commonalities between the five human "instinctive factors" as described by Völuspá s. 17-18 and the ones described in Jung's "The Structure and Dynamics of the Psyche" pp. 115–118. This fourth section also comments on Völuspá s. 31 mistletoe as Baldr's killer, with the help of Jung's interpretation of Frigg's role in "Symbols of Transformation" pp. 257–260. Völuspá is overflowing with examples of such "supra-individual universality" that Jung decided later to call the now famous "collective unconscious" (cf. note 8, p. 177 of 'Symbols…'). Extracting all of them would be an overwhelming task we are unable to carry out in this book, though we will deal with a few of them.

A fifth section comments on the appearance of mistletoe in Völuspá s. 31. It recalls and moderates C. G. Jung's description of Frigg as an archetypical 'Terrible Mother'.

IV-1. 'Active introspection' archetype

In § I-2.7.2 we already underlined that s. 28 and 141 both express a 'consciousness of being conscious' as do s. 18 and 138.

Hávamál 18	Pseudo-English literal translation
Sá einn veit	Who the one is mindful [*or* aware, conscious]
er víða ratar	who far travels
ok hefr fjöld of farit,	and raises [*or:* starts] much of 'for travelling',
hverju geði	**what state of mind**
stýrir gumna hverr,	leads the men such that [leads such men],
sá er vitandi er vits.	who is 'being mindful' is [*or:* he who] 'of *or* towards mindfulness'

Intelligent Robotics have been repeatedly tripping over the lack of self-conscience of computer programs. They recognize this problem as stemming from the robots' lack of "meta-thinking." This way of speech follows from Data Analysis that uses meta-data (i.e. data about the data) in order to help the user of a database to become conscious of the kind of knowledge stored in the data.

It is clear that the coexistence of knowledge and meta-knowledge inside the human brain looks like contradictory. The contradiction has been well exemplified by a French philosopher of the beginning of the 20th century, called Alain (Émile Chartier). He would claim that introspection is absurd because "you cannot be on the balcony looking down at yourself walking in the street." On the opposite, in this stanza, though without using the same words, Óðinn suggests that being conscious of one's conscience, i.e. something very similar to introspection, is the expected result of life experience for a human thoughtful person.

We however need to add that this Computer Science way of speech provides only a static view of what is "to be conscious of one's conscience." For the time being, there is no way to program data bases each element of which could be 'conscious' of (i.e. able to interact with) all other elements in the base. As explained in our technical papers with M. Franova (2017 and 2019), this kind of symbiosis would demand to represent the database through a non primitive recursive function, which cannot be but approximated. Inversely, one human thinking feature is the ability of our ideas to interact with each other, and this interaction is able to be the source of other new ideas, as stated by Óðinn in s. 18 and several other Hávamál stanza as we shall see.

Note that Óðinn, who so often criticizes human-like stupidity, does not call stupid or non-wise people those who are unable to analyze by their own thought the way they think. He rather marvels at the existence of such "state of mind" in s. 18, line 4.

It is not so strange that the line "*sá er vitandi er vits*," as underlined by Evans (1986), caused so much confusion among commentators because it looks so apart from 'standard' Hávamál other lines. It is quite true that, often, words used by Óðinn describe everyday behaviors, such as for example stanzas 11-14 dedicated to alcohol consumption. On the occasion, he may evoke obvious psychological consequences of these behaviors, such as for example the memory loss caused by excess drinking. Until s. 28, he never tackled with the topic of human thought functioning, that we can call 'human mental reality', i.e. his/her psyche. As soon as s. 28, however, Óðinn insists on the importance of practicing *vitandi er vits*, i.e. conscious to be conscious. This could be looked upon by many as an unbearable snobbish intellectualism ... though such a blame applied to the 'Víking' civilization is slightly preposterous. Conversely, as long human **activity** is an essential humankind's characteristic according to Völuspá s. 17, we need to accept Óðinn's recommendation of being thoughtful of the why and the how of our thinking and of our actions.

In order to avoid lengthy discussions on what conscience really is, for us and Óðinn, let us propose a single discriminant feature that does not claim to exhaust the topic of self-awareness, though it will be enough for us to illustrate how this *vitandi er vits* is already a contact with the concept of infinity. Note that here 'infinity' here does not always entails a huge number: it means that there is no way to predict when the generative process will stop. Since a human being cannot easily handle infinity, it is obvious that he/she will have tendency to either becoming confused, or his/her thought turn in circles when thinking of the infinite. This may be what explains the subjacent popular irony caused by those who acknowledge practicing introspection. On the contrary, in the present stanza, Óðinn says he admires this form of meditative mind as long as it avoids being trapped in his/her meditation by interacting with another intelligence, and when some useful conclusions can be drawn from it.

Now, in order to take into account the importance of action in Old Norse thinking, let us state that it is a form of introspection which is not limited to the observation of one's own mind, but which draws the conclusions of its observations as for the way of acting. We will call "active introspection" this kind of conscience of our conscience. Here is very simple example of such a behavior. Suppose that someone always appeared antipathetic to us and that we later become aware that he/she has many common features with a person we appreciate. It then becomes possible that we decide to revise our opinion on him/her. This may then initiate series of actions and thoughts of which we will be conscious and that, in turn, will encourage other awakenings. This illustrates how active introspection may possibly generate an endless ('infinite') number of ideas and actions.

Two other stanzas, 20 and 27, though slightly obscure, strongly hint at what may happen to a person who is self-unaware.

Hávamál s. 20	**Pseudo-English literal translation**
Gráðugr halr,	The greedy [*or* gluttonous] man
nema geðs viti,	unless (if of his) spirits would be conscious
etr sér aldrtrega;	he eats [*metaphoric meaning*: he consumes] self for (his) difficult time; [*also*: deadly sorrow]

These three lines suggest that a too greedy person will eat him/herself to death unless he/she is conscious of his/her mind.

Hávamál 2	**Pseudo-English literal translation**
1. *Ósnotr maðr*	A <u>non-wise human</u>
2. *er með aldir kemr,*	who with others comes
3. *þat er bazt, at hann þegi;*	that is best, for him to stay silent;
4. *engi þat veit,*	none who knows
5. *at hann ekki kann,*	at him non can [that he can nothing]
6. *[nema hann mæli til margt;]*	except he (that he) speaks very much;
7. *veit-a maðr*	knows-not a human
8. *hinn er vettki veit,*	he who nothing knows
9. *[þótt hann mæli til margt.]*	in spite of that he speaks very much

The classical interpretation of this stanza is an apology in favor of silence and that an unwise (or ignorant) person reveals him/herself by speaking too much. The last three lines, however seem to introduce the idea that this person who speaks too much does not know that he knows nothing. In other word, he is unable to observe his own ignorance, a negative version of the importance of self-knowledge. In a sense, if there is here an apology in favor of silence, it does advise first to be careful in communicating with other ones and, second, to take good care to communicate with one self.

This leads us to the following four remarks.

Firstly, s. 27 is related to 18 which declares that out-of-norm persons (possibly magicians) have a 'form of spirit' such as they are *vitandi er vits*, i.e. their spirit is conscious of itself. This comment leads to the awareness of a link with s. 18, i.e. with introspection.

Secondly, s. 27 applies to a non-wise person. Especially in view of 18, we can suppose that it describes the 'non behavior' of a wise person. This non-wise person is unable to realize that his excessive speech is nothing but the one of a super parrot that can utter a limited number of sentences. These sentences are more or less out of tune since life brings us in an infinite variety of contexts that must be described by an infinite number of ideas. The wise one is not submitted to such a limitation and his/her sentences will always be perfectly adapted to the current context.

Thirdly, though a bit aside from our main line of argumentation, note that our conclusions are more than "pure speculation" as specialists so often state. Instead of treating Hávamál as a set of disconnected stanzas, we use here the links between various stanzas to build up our argument.

The fourth remark brings us back to the problem of magic in Eddaic Poetry.

Intermezzo: A curse (not so much) hidden in Hávamál s. 27

It is well known that Eddaic magic makes use of special poetical structure called 'magic-meter' or rather 'incantation-meter' (Galdralag). At first sight, this stanza looks like a set of three consecutive groups in the classical Ljóðaháttr[7] style, as indicated in the ON version of s. 27 above. Remember that a really 'classical' Ljóðaháttr is made of six lines and not nine. We however cannot miss that lines 6 and 9 are almost identical in form and in meaning. Looking a bit closer at line 4 (*engi þat veit,*) and line 7 (*veit-a maðr*) we see they carry similar meanings: in line 4 "*engi veit,*" is a negation of '*veit*' and in line 7 "*veit-a*" is also a negation of '*veit*'. What happens with lines 5 and 8 is a bit different: the sound of "*hann ekki*" alliterates strongly with the one of "*hinn vettki*" and the meaning of "*kann*" (is able to do) of line 5 calls to action, while the verb of line 8 "*veit*" (knows) calls to reflection. In this case, "*kann*" and "*veit*" complete each other more than they repeat each other. This indicates that lines 7, 8 and 9 are interchangeable except the small though meaningful difference between '*kann*' and '*veit*'. This suggests that the six first lines of this stanza constitute a perfect Ljóðaháttr followed by a Galdralag as follows:

1. *Ósnotr maðr*
2. *er með aldir kemr,*
3. *þat er bazt, at hann þegi;*

4. *engi þat veit,*
5. *at hann ekki kann,*
6. *nema hann mæli til margt;*

repetition of 6: 6'. *nema hann mæli til margt;*
7. *veit-a maðr*
8. *hinn er vettki veit,*
9. *þótt hann mæli til margt.*

---

[7] Ljóða-háttr (of a song-short story) made of a Fornyrðislag to which is added a third line that must contain three alliterating syllables.

A repetition of line 6, say 6', produces a 'magic' reproduction of line 6, in the form of a Galdralag suggested by the upper part of the stanza, as above.

The same 'magic effect' can be obtained without repetition by clustering the lines as, for instance, (1, 2, 3) (4, 5) (6, 7, 8, 9) which suggest that the stanza could be recited several times with various clusters and various stressed syllables up to building a complex incantation.

This means that Hávamál s. 27 not only is, as classical commentators say, an apology in favor of silence for non-wise ones, it is more: a curse sent as sköp against non-wise characters who are not able to stay silent. Stanza 27 is often looked upon as being slightly trivial (because being incomprehensibly repetitive) while it provides us a hint at how Old Norse magic might have been 'slyly' included in the poems.

End of intermezzo

Let us now compare Hávamál s. 28 and s. 63:

S. 27 describes a 'non-wise human' and prepares us to s. 28 and 63 describing an individual who "believes to be knowledgeable" by including a new function of human's mind, one is (potentially) able to generate an infinite number of ideas and actions by the means of interactions among humankind.

Hávamál 28 (3 first lines)	Pseudo-English literal translation
Fróðr sá þykkisk,	Learned so self-think
er fregna kann,	who ask questions can,
*ok segja it **sama**;*	and speak it together;

and

Hávamál 63	Pseudo-English literal translation
Fregna ok segja	Ask and say
skal fróðra hverr,	shall of the wise ones who,
sá er vill heitinn horskr;	he who will be named wise;
einn vita	one only (should *or* could) know,
né annarr skal,	no other one shall (know),
þjóð veit, ef þrír ro.	the (whole) people know it, if three are (aware of it).

These two stanzas use the expression ***fregna ok segja*** which means 'to question and say' but stanza 28 adds ***sama***, which leads to the understanding "to pronounce both the questions and the answers." We thus understand that the three first lines of s. 28 are ironical since who enunciates the questions and the answers is ridiculous. Conversely, the three first lines of 63 are laudatory, the subject is able to converse with him/herself or with someone else, and to express an opinion in the form of a discussion that enriches the knowledge of both.

An interesting example of a similar behavior is provided by Völuspá s. 29 that describes how the völva, by teaching "magic fates and the art of prediction" to Óðinn (i.e. while answering his questions), "still and still widened her vision of this Earth" (possibly by questioning him back or communicating with him in some other way).

The secrecy surrounding the possibly magic knowledge, as suggested by the last three lines of s. 63, is a mark of its importance and its danger. This strongly states that magic knowledge can be misused with catastrophic effects for the sorcerer's apprentice and his/her experimental subjects.

The expression *regna ok segja* is illustrated in Eddaic poetry by higher beings whose main motivation is an insatiable need for more knowledge, such are for example Óðinn, and the völva he questions in Völuspá. Their knowledge unceasingly increases and evolves.

Increasing knowledge performs in a way similar to introspection for action (as defined in § IV-1 s. 18 commentaries) that self-analyses and generates new forms of conscience.

Both knowledge growth and introspection for action require that the learner interacts with the physical universe and/or with another human person. The only difference between the two is that 'thirst for knowledge' is satisfied only by an exchange between two human having different knowledge, whereas active conscience works in introspection for action. None of them poses a limit to their extension which explains that they offer an image of a possible infinity.

Hávamál 95 paraphrases on a similar theme by telling us that intelligence and feelings ("the village of the heart") are closely linked together and concluding that lack of self-agreement is the worse for the 'wise ones':

Hugr einn þat veit
er býr hjarta nær,
*einn er **hann** sér um sefa;*
öng er sótt verri
hveim snotrum manni
en sér engu að una.

Pseudo-English literal translation	**One possible translation**
Mind (intelligence) one (alone) what knows	Thought alone knows what
is the village of the heart near,	is close to the village of the heart,
one-alone is **he** to **him-self**;	**he** is alone to **himself** in his soul;
nothing that sickness might-be	nothing (is similar to) a disease
for-all wise human-ones	for each wise one
but in one-self with-nothing at feeling-good.	as being in self-agreement about nothing.

(nothing worse for a wise one than self-disagreeing about everything)

The pronoun *hann* means 'he' or 'him' in the masculine nominative and accusative. Evans supposes that it is impossible that this 'he' (in bold letters in the literal translation) refers to *hugr* which is however a masculine. This leads him to conclude that the wise one (male) is alone in his heart. Most translators think as Evans does, except (at least) Orchard who translates line 3 by "alone it (mind) sees into the soul." Orchard's choice preserves the importance of a self-conscious mind, and it keeps the welcome ambiguity relative to the gender of the wise one. The classical understanding, on the contrary, implies the commentators' belief that those primitive pirates ('*víkingar*') have been unable to use introspective thinking in order analyze their heart.

Magic and faith are so intimately intertwined in the Norse civilization that it is quite possible that Old Norse people would treat them as one single manifestation of their spiritual life, as suggested by famous and so much commentated stanza:

Hávamál 138.	Pseudo-English literal translation
Veit ek, at ek hekk	Know I, that I hung
vindgameiði á	windy-pole-tree on
nætr allar níu,	nights all nine,
geiri undaðr	by a spear wounded
ok gefinn Óðni,	and given to Óðinn,
sjalfur sjalfum mér,	self to self-mine,
á þeim meiði.	on it pole-tree.

The way of speech: "given to Óðinn, self to self-mine" could well express a powerful image of the 'social-magic' Norse Archetype liking together their socially 'active introspection' and what can be dubbed as their 'active faith'. It also evokes s. 18 *"vitandi er vits,"* where the central being is him/herself the object of attention. What these twisted formulas may exactly mean?

The answer to this question asks for a tight analysis of the differences between our present unconscious archetype of 'life and death' and the one of the ancient Norse people. In this book, we analyzed all the Eddaic stanzas dealing with explicit magic, not the ones dealing with the 'life and death' unconscious archetype. Thus, no well-checked information on this topic is really available to us: another full book would be needed to provide a reliable answer. On the top of this, the present book author must confess that he still feels slightly (though relatively) too young to be able to deal with such a deep topic. This is why the next section will provide nothing but a tentative answer, though it is based on mostly 'well known' facts about Old Norse worldview on 'life and death'.

IV-2. A modest try at unveiling some aspects of the Norse 'Life-and-Death' archetype

This section endeavors to find a partial explanation of the deep meaning of two Hávamál ways of speech included in s. 18 and 138, *"vitandi er vits* ([to be] conscious to be conscious)" and "*(gefinn) sjalfr sjalfum mér* (given self to self-mine)."

In the context of a Christocentric civilization, we will immediately recognize the Christian mystics who offered themselves to Christ and, simultaneously, spot here an "obvious Christian influence."

Ancient Norse ('Viking' and 'pre-Viking') civilization however existed in the context of an ancestors' religion the base of which is similar to an euhemerism, i.e. in which the gods could be particularly famous ancestors. This is consistent with the well-known old Norse family based religion. This means that each person was, on the one hand devoted to his/her dear departed ancestors and, on the other hand knew that after his/her death, depending on his/her fame, he/she will also become an honored 'dear departed'. It follows that each person was in charge to build up by him/herself an amount of good repute out of which his/her children would draw their devotion for this person when she/he will be dead. In other words, faith and repute were both to be built during each one's life. This is illustrated by famous Hávamál stanza 76:

Deyr fé...	Die riches...
en orðstír	but good fame
deyr aldregi	never dies
hveim er sér góðan getr.	for whom honestly gets it.

which insist on the point that this fame has to be honestly won.[8]

Manly pride at being faithful to one's words is attested by saga literature and by runic inscriptions that recall how much 'faithful' the deceased has been. A similar feminine pride has been less obvious until the publication, in 2002, of a collection of papers untitled "Cold Counsel—Women in Old Norse Literature and Mythology" dedicated to Lotte Motz by the editors of this book. These papers illustrate how a good number of sagas describe

---

[8] The idea that Norse individuals may put more importance in one's family honor than in his/her own preservation is not shared by all specialists. The following citation illustrates how much Old Norse ethics might be misunderstood: "The ideology of this poet's view of survival after Ragnarök seems simple and clear-cut: it is an amoral matter (as, indeed, most Norse heathenism seems to have had rather little to do with ethics) and the things which will ensure survival ... will not ensure one's survival, but only that of one's family; and that is an inadequate consolation in the face of one's own inevitable death." (John McKinnel, *Essays on eddic poetry*, Toronto Press, 2014, p. 167–8). It is clear that McKinnel attributes here to an Old Norse person either his own fears of death or what he believes to be normality in our modern civilization.

women taking charge of the family fame in front of timid males who have been shy at taking revenge and they are hassling them with "cold counsels" thus pushing them into a deadly vendetta. In this case, it may be that 'cold counsel' is an unfortunately negative choice of words: "keeping family repute" may be nearer to the target.

A more individual example of male and female pride in front of death is found in Sigurðarkviða in skamma (Short song of Sigurd) which actually describes all the breached oaths within Sigurðr's story. As we shall see now, all these violators loudly claim they always have been faithful to their oaths.

In s. 17, when Gunnarr's four sons start complotting against Sigurðr with whom they are linked by a brotherhood oath:

Old Norse	**Textually**	**Larrington**
1. Einu því Högni	Alone to that Högni (*answered*)	Hogni replied, he had a single answer:
1'. slíkt at vinna,	In such way to work	"It is not fitting for us to do this,
2. sverði rofna	by sword to be broken	with a sword
3. svarna eiða,	swore oath,	cutting asunder
3'. eiða svarna,	oath swore,	the oaths we've sworn,
2'. unnar tryggðir.	plighted faithfulness.	the pledges made."

Caroline Larrington splendidly provided a comprehensible version that perfectly renders the meaning of the Old Norse version … at the price of killing its magic content. As in the § just above we find here some magic called by repetition of 'almost the same' lines in Hávamál s. 24. In Sigurðarkviða in skamma s. 17, lines 1 and 1' read as a classical Fornyrðislag,[9] as well as lines 2 and 2', while 3 and 3' carry the Galdralag,[10] here embedded between the two lines of the second Fornyrðislag.

In that case, it seems that Högni warns his accomplices, namely Gunnar and Guðórm that their proposal of killing Sigurðr is prone to bring some

---

[9] A Fornyrðis-lag is an 'of ancient-poetical meter' the oldest and simplest one made of sequences of pairs of alliterating verses, each of them contains 2 stressed syllables. [Recall: We have already seen a third kind of eddic verses, the Ljoða-háttr (of a song-short story) made of one Fornyrðislag to which is added a third line that must contain three alliterating syllables.]

[10] A Galdra-lag is an 'of magic song-poetical meter'. It is an irregular sequence of intensely alliterating verses associated to 'almost' identical sequences of verses.

(cursing) sköp upon them. But Guðórm is young enough for being unconcerned by these pledges and Gunnarr asks him to be Sigurðr's killer … which is not really compatible with these pledges! Anyhow, Guðórm puts a sword in Sigurðr's heart while he his sleeping with his wife Guðrún. Guðórm is instantly killed ('every one' knows that he is split in two from head to legs) by Sigurðr who actually dies nine stanzas later. Before dying, Sigurðr states that he did no harm to Gunnarr, thus

> … *síðr værak heitinn*   … little may I be called (hardly can I be called)
> *hans kvánar vinr.*   of his wife friend. (a friend of his wife)

which expresses that he never cheated Gunnarr. This is perhaps factually true but 'everyone also knows' how much Gunnarr's wife, on her side, has been deeply in love with Sigurðr … it is clear that, at least, Gunnarr had good grounds to feel cheated. Besides, stanza 40 tells that she loved a single man during her life, namely Sigurðr:

> *Unnak einum*   I acknowledge (or love) one only,
> *né ýmissum,*   not with 'alternations', (a particularly delicate way
>   of saying 'unfaithfulness')
> *bjó-at of hverfan*   dwelled-not 'turned-around' (fickle)
> *hug men-Skögul;*   mind the necklace-Skögul (a Valkyrie).
>   [Never a fickle mind inhabited the Valkyrie of the
>   necklace.]

In s. 47, she has a last look on all her 'goods', including her (killed) servants. She then puts on her most beautiful golden mail-coat and "pierce herself with her sword". As well as Sigurðr (or even better than him), she dies quite slowly. In the following 23 stanzas she tells of the future of those that are watching her death. In the last two lines of the last stanza she claims in a last breath that she always had been sincere:

> … *satt eitt sagðak,*   what I said I did say (I said what I had to say)
> *svá mun ek láta.*   then must I leave.

The 'active faith' of all these proud people, as well as Brunildr's, is built on a daily effort in winning or preserving one's good repute, even if a slightly disputable one. Inversely, some other religions grant faith to their followers by a revelation delivered by God or his prophets or his Churches: this faith is essentially 'given', not essentially won.

Old Norse faith is active because "to be offered to oneself" is a mental act that has to be carried out over the years and which uses the rules of active conscience defined in § IV-1 s. 18 commentaries. It differs from a more passive faith which might have been revealed by a kind of miracle and not obtained by the way of an obstinate work.

IV-3. Ragnarök archetype

As a simplified way of speech, we have until now seen Ragnarök as being a "Nordic Apocalypse" as understood in this book in § III-1. If we remember that an eschatology is classically defined as "the part of theology concerned with death, judgement, and the final destiny of humankind," and that an Apocalypse tells of the final phase of an eschatology, we may note that these two words exclusively deal with humankind. Our point his not to recall that many other living species could be considered. Our point is recalling that Ragnarök mostly deals with the destiny of gods. That is why it looks slightly illogical to speak of a Norse eschatology unless we accept the euhemeristic trick stating that Northern gods are not 'real gods' but real historical persons. This attitude is possible though it implicitly treats the Northern gods as Christian individuals while they are defined as pagan entities.

In other words, we spot here the presence of two different images of a common archetype, the one of Religion where the capital R is used in order to single out its archetypical state. The Christian image of Religion entails a Christian eschatology adopted by a vast majority of ancient Norse texts readers. On their side, the pagan Norse people, by including the gods in their 'pseudo-eschatology', developed another image of Religion. Let us now try to somewhat deeper analyze how the Norse 'unique' feature of Ragnarök might be linked to the Norse worldview.

At first it may be necessary to explain that the Norse "ancestor's religion," though based on ancestors' worship, thus related to a kind of euhemerism, is far from being a naïve belief. The sagas do report naïve beliefs such as banquets with the ancestors in remote locations and complex relationships between the living and the living-dead ones (called *draugar* or *haugbúar*). These relations are discussed in 'Quiet Draugar' (see bibliography). The most beautiful and touching of such relations is described in Hervara ok Heiðreks saga, translated as 'Heiðreks saga' in Larrington's new translation of the Poetic Edda (2014, Oxford U. Press, pp. 268–273). A commented translation of this poem is also available at 'Hervör's myth' (see bibliography). If we now look what happens during Ragnarök, we get nothing more than the dry information that "death is death, and that's it" as implied by Völuspá s. 52 (last 4 lines) saying nothing more optimistic than:

"rocks hit one another
and monsters travel,
mankind walks on the way to Hel
and the sky cleaves."

This conclusion does not much stirs imagination and we can thus understand why it has been seemingly been forgot by the saga tellers.

The above information is totally the reverse of the one of pre-Ragnarök times as illustrated by Hávamál s. 76 that delivers the famous statement: "repute never dies, that which is obtained by being good and honest." This implicitly states that each living offspring will preciously and lovingly keep along the repute of his/her ancestors, something certainly unexpected in the present way of life. We now may hypothesize that the huge mounts nearby ancient *hallir* are not what we call 'tombs' in which the famous deceased would live forever or wait for going to some heaven, as suggested by a Christian worldview. They are, as so many runes inscribed standing stones say, pleas to an 'eternal till Ragnarök' remembrance of illustrious ancestors or appreciated "good fellows." This suggests the existence of a 'Norse eternity' referring to a lapse of time that is very different from both a 'Christian infinity' and the modern one, such the 'for ever and ever' definition given by Wikipedia. It might be better understood as a 'Norse long duration', i.e. an indeterminate presumably long span of time, the duration of which is unknown but strictly finite.

During a long period of several centuries, however, we know that the domination of a given family did not last forever since so many majestic longhouses have been burned, denoting major changes in the dominating families. This enable us to conjecture that Norse individuals observing the rise, decline and finally replacement of the most powerful families, have been brought to imagine 'the duration of one single family' as being a relatively short example of their 'Norse very long durations', i.e. each great family disappearance provides a small example of what Norse long durations might look like. This brings us back to the concept of 'noble ancestors' as divine individuals whose divine status were bound to disappear someday, and this exactly fits the concept of Ragnarök.

All this might be an explanation of the intimate relationship between a respected 'ancestor religion' and an expected Ragnarök.

IV-4. Two strong archetypal images + Twice five "instinctive factors"

(Völuspá s.17 and s.18)

IV-4.1. Forewords

As above in § IV-1, the archetypal image we shall now define is born from a deep difference between pagan and Christian world views. When Völuspá s. 17 and s. 18 describe how three Æsir created humankind, their actions and godly gifts are identical for both future beings, male and female. This underlines the existence of two widely different images for a common archetype we can call Humankind Creation.

The pagan image illustrates a humankind in which male and female members are essentially identical ('equal' to each other) at the time of their conception, notwithstanding future differences due the social context in which they live. Many other religions, including Christianity, propose an image of Humankind Creation in which, on the contrary, male and female members have been shaped as being essentially different ('non equal' to each other) at the time of their conception, notwithstanding possible future common features due the social context in which they live.

In other words, Norse pagans did carry inside them an essentially equaling sex image of Humankind Creation, as opposed to Christian ones who, during the Christianization process, had shaped in them an essentially sex differentiated image of Humankind Creation. These images belonging to their "collective unconscious," they are able to drive individuals to actions and conceptions that they feel being 'natural ones' some driven by an unconscious equalitarian worldview, the others by an unconscious non-equalitarian worldview, and both claiming that their behavior is the natural one. Note that being aware of this difference may slightly modify our behavior though their unconscious push cannot be avoided.

IV-4.2. *Norse image of the Creation of Mankind and its five urges for life*

Völuspá s. 17 and 18 describe how the gods created humankind. Stanza 17 provides two features defining a not yet human one as follows: the shapes that will become the first humans and let us recall that Ask and Embla are still "little having might" and "örlög-less."

s. 17

lítt megandi	6. little having might
Ask ok Emblu	7. Ask(r) and Embla
örlöglausa	8. örlög-less (deprived of örlög).

It is quite easy to realize that 'having no might' is a negatively expressed image for 'being able to act'. It follows that 'needing to act' is said to be one of primitive behaviors for a Norse person. It is quite obvious that 'power' represents being active and that 'being able to act' or the 'need to act' is one of our fundamental impulses.

In the same way, carrying one's örlög is pointed at as one of the primitive needs of a Norse person.

S. 18 states that three gods created two first human persons by providing them breath, intelligence, the internal water of our flesh and the beautiful color of our skin.

s. 18

önd *gaf Óðinn,*	5. breath gave Óðinn
óð gaf Hœnir,	6. intelligence gave Hœnir
lá gaf Lóðurr	7. 'sea' (water or blood) gave Lóðurr
oc lito góða.	8. and beautiful hue.

The way of speech in line 7 of s. 18 can be understood if we know that three of the Æsir had already created our universe from primitive giant Ymir's body, and that the oceans were formed from his blood. In s. 18, naming blood as 'sea' is a *heiti*, a classic style figure in skaldic poetry. Thus the 'sea' provided by Lóðurr to humans represents our blood which indeed gives us 'beautiful hue'.

As in s. 17, the gods' gifts can be considered as unconscious impulses conditioning the Norse way of life. Blood and beautiful hue embody our drive towards a healthy happy life, intelligence embodies our need to think, to speculate about our ways of living, and breath embodies life itself.

A touching instance of the vital role of breath is given by Sigurðarkviða in skamma s. 24-29 where Guðrún is said to wake up on the side of a dying Sigurðr (whose heart has just been stabbed by Guðórm) and who is still able cut his killer in two pieces and, after that dies 'inside' her beloved one's breath: "*Kona varp **öndu**, en konungr fjörvi* (The queen 'threw' **a breath**, and the king died)."

IV-4.3. Carl Jung's five 'basic instincts'

We just told of five basic impulses of the ancient Norse that belong to a very general archetype named Creation of Mankind. It turns out that in his book on the structure of the psyche (**C. G. Jung, "The Structure and Dynamics of the Psyche," Sections 236–246, pp. 116–118, Routledge 1960**), Carl Jung defines five 'basic instincts' that structure our unconscious. These are 1. hunger, 2. sexual need, 3. the need to act, 4. (active) thinking and 5. creativity.

If we refer to these Jung's five basic instincts, we will see that

1. Völuspá ranks first the need to act which obviously fits perfectly with Jung's third need. (Let us forget about örlög for the time being.)
2. Völuspá ranks third breath (Óðinn's gift) which embodies strength of life instinct, that is Jung's hunger and sexual need (and all survival instincts left implicit by Jung).
3. It ranks fourth intelligence, the intelligence that enables reflection, again obviously comparable to Jung's active thinking.
4. Völuspá ranks second owning örlög which finds no equivalent concept in Jung's list, and Jung ranks fifth 'creativity' which find no obvious correspondence in Völuspá.

This description underlines a large difference between Norse and modern thinking, as stressed by both ancient Norse Völuspá and modern C. Jung:

– 'a' – Örlög looks like a kind of private Norse feature, and
– 'b' – creativity looks like a private modern feature.

As for difference 'a' a large amount of this book strives at making örlög understandable to modern thinking, and the following will implicitly assume this has been successful.

In a few words, let us state again that Norse örlög are Norns edicts, unchangeable rules driving each and all human beings from their birth until their death. These rules nevertheless do not cover all details of our lives: this leaves kind of 'holes' within the örlög rules. Magic (most often human or godly sköp) may introduce in our destiny features that may modify particulars events of our lives.

As for difference 'b', in the following, we will try to characterize what might have been a possible Norse creativity, seen as a part of their intellect.

IV-4.4. *Hávamál s. 141 on "intellectual fertility"*

After telling in s.140 that he has been taught "nine powerful songs" by his grand-father Bölþorn and that he obtained "a full mouthful of the precious mead," Óðinn explains the changes he could observe on himself. They were: (*s. 141*)

Þá nam ek frævask	Then became I fertile
ok fróðr vera	and full of knowledge was
ok vaxa ok vel hafask,	and grew and well throve,
orð mér af orði	a word, out of my speech,
orðs leitaði,	of a word sought help,
verk mér af verki	a deed out of my deed
verks leitaði.	sought a deed.

Verb *frjóva*, here in the form *fræva*, means 'to bloom' and when reflexive it means 'to be fertile', i.e. 'usefully creative'.

(Myself out of myself, myself looks for help, I looked for help inside me), out of my own words and out of my own deeds.

This kind of creativity is not 'given by the gods' but self-acquired—visibly at a great expense of will. It takes fully into account Jung's creativity as long as s. 141 illustrates the ability and need to increase our intellectual activity, i.e. a process that demands creativity, and thus fulfils some kind of internal urge for creativity.

IV-4.5. *Achieving one's örlög*

Since ancient Norse knew that some örlög was allotted to each living creature, then the necessity of soon or late death was a strong image and since the gods were also submitted to their örlög, then the death of the gods was a natural thing, deeply imbedded in their collective archetypes. This prevent us to see in Ragnarök a more or less believable nebulous legend.

Ragnarök is a part of the five unconscious primary drives that governed ancient Nordic life, deeply encased in their unconscious thinking. The same has been holding for the Norse gods as shown by some myths about which one wonders why such powerful and intelligent beings committed some absurd blunders, without any reason than the necessity of fulfilling their örlög. For example, one wonders why on earth the Æsir felt compelled to cheat a little in the execution of their contract with Skaði to prevent her from marrying Baldr, as explained in the following 'far-fetched intermezzo'.

A far-fetched intermezzo on Æsir cheating Skaði

As we know, a female warrior, Giantess Skaði, requested to marry one of the Æsir as a wergild for her father's (Giant Þjazi) killing while Loki recovered Íðunn from her abduction by Þjazi (see Snorri's Skáldskaparmál, Ch. 1). Her gild included that she could decide on her chosen one while watching the candidates. For an unknown reason, it seems that the Æsir guessed that she would choose Baldr and, for yet another unknown reason, they disliked this issue. When the choice had to take place, they cheated on their oath by a play on the words based on the grounds that Skaði did not make precise that she wanted to look at them 'entirely' during the choice.

The Æsir thus felt entitled to ask Skaði to choose while seeing their feet only. It happens that Njörðr featured the most beautiful feet and she chose him. Our mythology speaks at length of the problems that this choice led to, though not of the consequences brought by her not marrying Baldr. It is not difficult to believe that, she being an accomplished warrior would have protected her beloved husband and might have countered in some way Loki's plot leading to Baldr's death … thus preventing, at least for the 'time being', the impending Ragnarök.

This interpretation may look far-fetched though it does answer the question: but why on earth did the Æsir choose to commit a serious breach to their own spirituality, that is to cheat on such a sworn contract?

IV-5. Baldr's death and Frigg's 'Terrible Mother' features

In case you do not know of Baldr's Dream, you will find a version of this myth at http://www.nordic-life.org/nmh/BaldrsDream.pdf.

Baldr's death is evoked in Völuspá s. 31, 32 and 33 and brings forward a striking hidden feature of Norse spirituality. Before going into this, as a supplement to chapter III, we have to show that the text is really pagan and that its meaning would be spoiled by a Christocentric understanding.

IV-5.1. Do not confuse Christ and Baldr

Baldr's death is very often compared to Christ's one. Indeed, here are two unusual beings, loved by all, beautiful and bright, endowed with a powerful charisma who are killed while they are at the beginning of their lives. They look very similar at first sight. We shall now give a closer analysis of the course of their lives and thus realize that they embody two archetypal images that are completely opposite to each other.

Christ, though considered partially divine throughout his life, leads a human life among humans. He will have to die to achieve full deity status. Finally, his death announces a religious era that will last forever, even after Last Judgment.

Baldr's life runs in an opposite way. He is born a god and leads his life among the gods. He does not know anything about human condition—at least no myth describes him mingling with humans. After his death, despite the gods' frantic attempts, he will join human ones in Hel, and thus lose his divine status. Finally, his death illustrates that the gods are mortal and preludes Ragnarök. His death announces the end of a religious era centered around Óðinn, Freyr, Þórr and Freyja.

IV-5.2. Baldr's death and life

They are evoked in Völuspá s. 31 and first half of s. 32.

Old Norse	Translation
s. 31	
Ek sá Baldri,	I looked at Baldr
blóðgum tívur,	blood-covered divine being,
Óðins barni,	Óðinn's son,
örlög fólgin;	(his) örlög hidden;
stóð of vaxinn	was standing (fully) grown
völlum hæri	in the fields taller
mjór ok mjög fagr	slender and very beautiful
mistilteinn.	mistletoe.

Baldr is blood-covered because he has been killed by an arrow made of mistletoe. Frigg, Baldr's mother, had been afraid by her son's dreams and she concocted powerful sköp protecting him from harm of all natural elements, excepted mistletoe she believed to be too young to be submitted to such a strong sköp.

The second half of this stanza describes mistletoe as being tall in the fields, slender and beautiful. This tells us that the 'mistletoe' that killed Baldr cannot be 'our' *Viscum album* that grows on other trees, but another unknown plant. It thus shows no parasitic behavior as opposed to 'our mistletoe'.

Old Norse	Literal translation	English
s. 32 first half		
Varð af þeim meiði,	Was of this stick	This fateful stick
er mær (*mjór*) sýndiz,	that slim self-appeared	that looked slim
harmflaug hættlig,	as harm-flight dangerous	was actually a harm-missile
Höðr nam scióta.	Höðr learned to fling.	that Höðr learned to fling.

In s. 31, mistletoe is qualified as *mjór*, that is 'slim'. This word can take the form *mær* with the same meaning, as it does in s. 32. This obviously evokes the other meaning, more usual, of *mær*: 'young girl, maiden'. The poet wants to say that mistletoe exerts a form of attraction, similar to the one of a slim young girl. In this case, attraction is morbid since mistletoe is the tool of Baldr's death.

IV-5.3. *Jung's analysis of Baldr's and Frigg's örlög*

Frigg is a complex goddess whose Óðinn's wife status tends to shade that she is the main image of 'Earth'. Both sides are not simple and, within the myth of Baldr's death, described in the poem *Baldrs draumar*, her main role is the one of Earth. She is able to ask all earth creatures (except one) to avoid hurting her son though, as our material earth, she has her positive sides as a provider of riches and her negative sides when she brings about such disasters as earth shakes or volcanic eruptions. Her behavior during 'Baldr's death crisis' could be understood as simple display of these two sides of her personality. This however would be an oversimplification of the myth, forgetting to take into account its many details. This is why we will now resort to Jung's analysis of this myth and also comment some unsettling details of the myth he does not explain. In his analysis, Jung does not use the mistletoe presented in Völuspá as a non-parasitic plant. Its supposed parasitic feature has been explicitly used by Jung as being a component of the deepest part of Frigg's unconscious (the archetype 'shadow' in his vocabulary).

A summary of Jung's interpretation of mistletoe

After recalling the various pagan images of mistletoe, Jung says **"We are told that mistletoe was 'too young'; hence this clinging parasite could be interpreted as the child of the tree."** We see that Jung strictly sticks to the botanical mistletoe understanding, while this name could be a *heiti* for another tree.

This leads him to see Balder as **"puer æternus"** (child eternal) who **"only lives on and through the mother and can strike no roots in the world..."** We at once see that the Völuspá character cannot be this kind of 'mistletoe' since s. 31 says that it "was standing grown in the fields."

"He is ... only a dream of the mother... But why should the mistletoe kill Baldur since he is, in a sense, his sister or brother?" Jung concludes that **"The mistletoe, however, corresponds to the <u>shadow brother</u> ... whom the psychotherapist regularly meets as personification of the personal unconscious ... the shadow becomes fatal when there is too little vitality or too little consciousness in the hero for him to complete his heroic task."**

C. G. Jung, Symbols of Transformation,
sections 392–394, pp. 257–259

Nobody will be surprised that Jung attributes Frigg's mistakes to her unconscious side. Another strong hint in favor of his interpretation is that, when asked the question: "Why did you overlook to include mistletoe in the magic spells you uttered for Baldr's protection?" she could not provide a better answer than "mistletoe was too young" to be submitted to such a strong spell. This amounts to an "I do not really know," i.e. an "I do not know why" typical of an unconscious behavior.

Worse, Jung leaves implicit the well-known fact that she had a bizarre need to blabber with an unknown sorceress (who actually turned out to be Loki under disguise), thus revealing the one weakness of her magic spells, again a behavior unworthy of a great goddess, thus yet another unconscious blunder.

Since these blunders are typical of irrepressible manifestations of the unconscious, also attributed to 'complexes' in everyday language, the line of thought proposed by Jung is therefore hardly disputable, though it is strangely unrespectful of Frigg—if we look at it from a Norse pagan point of view as we are trying to do in this book.

We are thus faced here with a problem: What then might be this **"shadow brother"** who is so dangerous? It has only two possible solutions: either she deliberately programmed her son's death or her unconscious took the better on her, and Jung's interpretation of her 'crazy' blunders becomes all the more acceptable.

A parenthesis on Frigg and her 'shadow'

In the above citation C. Jung casually uses the concept of 'shadow' which is one of the basic archetypes he has defined in Jung (2016 pp. 183, 284, 123):

"… there are human figures that can be arranged under a series of archetypes, the chief of them being, according to my suggestion, the *shadow*, the *wise old man*, the *child* (including the hero), the *mother* ("Primordial Mother" and "Earth Mother") … and her counterpart the *maiden*, and lastly the *anima* in man and the *animus* in woman."

"The shadow personifies everything that the subject refuses to acknowledge about himself and yet is always thrusting itself directly or indirectly—for instance, inferior traits of character and other incompatible tendencies …"

"the inferior function [the shadow] is practically identical with the dark side of the human personality."

It is important to cite also Jung (1966, p. 153) where he states: "The devil is a variant of the "shadow" archetype, i.e. of the dangerous aspects of the unrecognized dark half of the personality."

This last citation underlines the fact that Jung's focus is the one of humankind, not the one of ancient gods: What might have been nearest to 'the devil' for Frigg will not be discussed here. Inversely, since the Northern gods have human traits, we may question what have been "the dangerous aspects of the unrecognized dark half of Frigg's personality."

By attributing a shadow to Frigg, or at least, following the euhemerism theory of Old Norse religions, Jung attributes to the she-hero upon which goddess Frigg is based a conscious side that she pushed back in her deepest unconscious whatever shaming incidents or feelings she might have had to suffer.[11]

---

[11] This recalls the end of Sigurðarkviða in skamma (§ II-12) where Brunhidr last words are in s.71:

ómun þverr,	a (my) voice dies out,
undir svella,	under (the effect of) swelling,
satt eitt sagðak,	truth one (the very truth) I declared
svá mun ek láta.	thus I will let go.

In her last words, she claims to have been always truthful while the very complexity of her life allows some doubts over this claim and this suggests that she might had have 'complexes' and that she unconsciously pushed down to her shadow-side these less glorious details.

This suggests that Jung's tracks, whatever anachronical they might look, will be useful to understand Frigg's strange behavior. The only reservation we have to point out is associated with the statement that Jung's 'shadow' is a strongly pejorative feature since it "is practically identical with the dark side of the human personality."

IV-5.4. *Mistletoe and Frigg's örlög*

We already underlined that each human person and each god or goddess is submitted to an örlög, and that he/she sooner or later will fulfill it. Frigg's behavior seems to have been driven by an unconscious power that looks very much like the ones of örlög, and in turn, her behavior caused Baldr's death, another way to suggest that it has been the hidden cause that triggered Ragnarök.

This interpretation however puts Frigg into the ridicule position of someone blundering due to a loss of consciousness. These blunders will be better understood if we realize that Völuspá s. 31-33 suggest a less menial cause to her behavior. When Mistletoe appears in Völuspá, Baldr is still a shadow in Hel, and Mistletoe would then be no more than a simple 'shadow of a shadow' though simultaneously a vivid young tree.

A possible understanding of the existence, exactly in the middle of Völuspá, of such an ironical arch-beautiful tree can be commented as follows: Mistletoe could be a duplicate of Yggdrasill, here presented as a young tree, as s. 2 presents Yggdrasill being still under the ground. Since Mistletoe is a representative of the unbound power of the Giants, it will grow in a world freed of the Æsir, thus with a role opposite to Yggdrasill's, that is, no longer as *mjöt-viðr* 'measure-giver tree' but as *hamstoli-viðr* (furious tree), a 'lack-of-control provider-tree' in a Giants' universe, distinct from the one of surviving Æsir and humans, one exclusively housing Giants.

We may now explain an implicit aspect of Norse mythology: C. Jung has been quite firm in seeing in Frigg a 'terrible mother' similar to some his clients. While keeping the same line as his, we notice that he never took into account Völuspá s. 31 that negates the belief that Norse 'mistletoe' is identical to the bush we call *Viscum album*, therefore negating also Jung's claim to identify it with Baldr's 'shadow', a very negative instance of what we could also see as a 'Baldr's component' of Frigg's animus, that is a much larger and complex unconscious among which Mistletoe has certainly a place together with many other unconscious components. We have observed that reducing Frigg to a 'terrible mother' does not fit with her 'great goddess' status in Norse mythology. We are now open to another way to understanding her behavior by looking at a less deprecating explanation.

Two main goddesses share the honor of representing most of the feminine side of Norse religion. One is Frigg and the other Freyja. This last one is clearly in charge of teaching magic and ensuring female fertility so as to preserve the future of the families worshipping her. On her side, Frigg is specifically in charge of earth magic (though she does not teach it) and of female pride, thus a Norse representation of the ancient 'Great Goddess' who reigned at least during Sumerian times under the name Inanna. Some two thousand years however separate Inanna's glory from Frigg's dignity. This loss of status as a representative of female pride is reflected in the two flaws that led to her son's death: Baldr himself behaving childishly by challenging the other gods to harm him and Frigg babbling out the one weakness in her protective magic. In both cases, we can assimilate what looks as a lack of consciousness to their örlög that took the better on their conscious and in Frigg's case, that even took the better on her worldwide sköp by which she hoped to protect her son.

Finally, the main difference between the 'primitive' Norse and a 'civilized' modern man reduces to that ancient Norse used to call örlög the urges of their unconscious they tended to accept while we, civilized ones, call unconsciousness the same urges we tend to fight or dismiss.

IV-5.5. *Mistletoe and Óðinn's örlög*

After Baldr's death, Óðinn undergoes a rigorous mourning as long as Höðr is not "killed and carried on a funerary burner" as says Völuspá s. 33:

Þó hann æva hendr	Though he never hands (washed)
né höfuð kembdi,	nor head combed
áðr á bál um bar	until on a pyre (*he*) carried
Baldrs andscota;	Baldr's enemy (Höðr).
Enn Frigg um grét	But Frigg wept
í Fensölum	in Fensalir
vá Valhallar–	the tragedy of Valhöll—
Vitoð ér enn, eða hvat?	You still want to know, and what?

Óðinn is in a situation with no real issue. He must avenge Baldr's death, and he is told that the only possible avenger is another of his sons whose mother must be the goddess Rindr. In short, to avenge the death of his son Baldr killed by his son Höðr, he must beget with Rindr a third son who will kill the second one. Since this third son will kill the second one to avenge the first one, Óðinn has no other choice than becoming himself the wergild of the second murder he supports. This directly leads him to Ragnarök where all debts will be erased. Loki's motivation to help Höðr to kill Baldr is not pure meanness: he knew he was building a deadly trap for Óðinn.

The following stanza, s. 34, speaking of the chains that will immobilize Loki, directly jumps to the punishment imposed on Loki by the Æsir, leaving aside 'details' of great importance.

34.

Þá kná Vála	Váli was however able
vígbönd snúa,	to twist battle-bonds
heldr vóro	that were rather
harðgerhöpt,	quite hard chains
ór þörmom.	(done) out of entrails.

Óðinn's duty to generate another 'brother killer' was quite well-known and we can suppose that the poet wanted to push his listeners to fill themselves the vacuum between s. 33 and s. 34. This stanza tells us that Váli is the one who twisted the bonds that hold Loki under the mouth of a serpent that let flow its poisoned spit on Loki. From other sources, we also know that Váli, son of Rindr, is also Höðr killer, i.e. Baldr's avenger. Óðinn has been warned that Baldr's avenger had to be a son that he had to beget with a woman named Rindr. He did then try to seduce Rindr, but she rejected him. After several unsuccessful attempts to seduce her, he will resort to cunning and it so happens that his duty to avenge Baldr will lead him to rape Rindr, adding a shameful behavior to the non-tractable situation in which he finds himself.

It turns out to be possible to compare Óðinn's 'pagan' distress to the similar one of a more Christianized king. The Anglo-Saxon poem Beowulf reports a case similar to the one we just described. However, the Anglo-Saxons were Christianized much before the Norse and Óðinn's parallel hero, Hreðel, will behave in a much less drastic way than Óðinn because he will simply wither away inside his dilemma. This episode is found in Beowulf lines 2435–2443. King Hreðel had two sons and, by unfortunate chance, one of them misses the target he is aiming at and kills "*broðor oðerne blodigan gare*" (a brother the other (with) a bloody shaft). Finally, the king recognizes that he can do nothing better than compose a

> "*sarigne sang, þonne his sunu* painful song, his son hanged,
> *hangaðhrefne to hroðre…*" a pleasure for ravens…

In other words, Hreðel gives up looking for an honorable exit to his dilemma besides whining about his sorrow. Óðinn certainly felt trapped within his örlög. He nevertheless went to his death in a really honorable way: he did wrong and unwailingly paid the price of his mistakes. We meet here a striking example of the difference between a pagan Norse worldview of and the one of an early convert to Christianity.

General Conclusions of This Book

Conclusion 1

The primary goal of this book has been to build the tools necessary to reveal some images of the Norse unconscious archetypes relative to various aspect of their worldviews, as embedded within their poetical production.

A preliminary step in order to fulfill this purpose, is to publicly underline the (mis)use of seemingly mundane words that should be interpreted as carrying magic. The most striking example is the mundane use of words associated to verb *skapa* (often translated by a dry 'to do') even though they belong to a 'not really mundane' context such as the gods 'doing' tools as soon as the years could be counted (Völuspá s. 7), or warriors who 'let grow the sköp' in Atlamál in grænlenzku s. 2 (see § II-17). It is clear that reading Eddaic poetry as dealing with mundane topics, if not a complete misunderstanding, reveals a deliberate choice for being blind to the role of magic within Old Norse civilization. Such a choice biases towards a commonplace version the poems expressing Old Norse spirituality. This spirituality may be sometimes hard to spot, hard to spot because the ancient Norse one is indeed very different from a Christian one.

Chapter II has provided a large number of such choices, in particular these that underline the importance of Yggdrasill as a cosmic orchestra conductor who measures the amount of power to allot to the various characters on the cosmic stage. That this 'supreme godly figure' might get burned during Ragnarök can be looked at from two different points of view.

One is the 'defeat' point of view that brings to believe (or fervently hope) in the existence of eternal things and beings, and need this belief to accept our transient human life. Ragnarök is then a kind of supreme tragedy for humankind, also called apocalypse.

The other one is the 'necessity' point of view, also illustrated by the belief in örlög and which acknowledges that the only eternal thing is the tight dependence of life to receive death and of death to be allotted life. Ragnarök is then a kind of last achievement for humankind. Many will find inadequate this view: this rejection simply follows from the deeply ingrained belief that we, humankind, should be eternal, a feeling that would perhaps be looked upon as a crazy fancy by the ancient Norse 'thinkers', i.e. the person involved in both mundane and magic knowledge who had been aware of Völuspá content. The new world (be it 'influenced' or not) hinted at in the seven last stanzas is so different from our 'good old' world and its description is so summary that it brings no relief to the upheaval related in the 58 preceding stanzas.

We nevertheless have to accept that, though we did weaken the belief in Christian influences, we were unable to 'prove' the absence of these influences. This negative statement is however limited by the fact that we chose the most brilliant academic production in favor of them (in this book: a part of it, see references to Völuspá below) and proving the weakness of their arguments, sometimes even going down to an intense awkwardness as those taking root in some obscure literature. This shows that we are still waiting for the Christianity inspired scholar who will develop really convincing arguments different from the somewhat late dating of written Eddaic poetry. Meanwhile, it is still safe to use, as we did here, this Pagan Edda as a reliable source of information relative to the Pagan Norse worldview.

Conclusion 2

We know that the authorization to privately practice Forn Siðr (Ancient Behavior or 'religion') in Iceland has been canceled around 1020, and thus Norse poetry was outlawed during some two centuries of intense Christianization before starting to be written down by Snorri Sturluson. It is nevertheless certain that the custom of asking a Thing 'Speaker' to recite the laws (some financing was even allotted to putative Speakers to get help in memorizing the whole corpus) has been pretty much preserved until Iceland became a Norwegian colony around 1282.

Using again a part of III – 2.2.5, let us say that, at least, one group of Icelanders had the ability to memorize texts much lengthier and more boring than the few thousand lines of a prestigious poetical corpus, often on purpose 'built' to stimulate memorization. The only possible explanation to this riddle is that some poetry antiquarian scholars protected (obviously at 'the best of their knowledge') versions of Hávamál, Völuspá and other poems from Christian influences and followed a tradition attested by Snorri Sturluson a few years before. Considering the observed failure to find properly arguable such influences, they have been indeed quite efficient.

They may not have been keeping the original version (which 'original' one? Quite probably several similar versions already existed in different locations during pagan times) but at least it retells the Forn Siðr these scholars still knew at the beginning of the 13th century … and they did carefully expunge their beloved Edda from all Christian influences, as implicitly explained in Chap. III! We can well imagine one or several groups of scholars, all knowing the poems of the Poetic Edda, disputing of what was the best versions and eliminating from each version what they felt to be a Christian influence in order to obtain the most 'authentic' possible pagan synthesis of the poem, the one we know. The content of chapter III shows that they did quite good job at it since all the 'influences' that have been detected by expert of the ON language are extraordinarily shallow and should never have been accepted in a really 'religion-neutral' academic community.

We also did our best to convince our readers of an Old Norse coexistence between religion, magic and way of life. Our modern world that never stops using a 'divide and conquer' strategy may be fundamentally deaf, blind and befuddled when facing a civilization that does not share the same thinking strategy.

Let us now observe how Norse infinity, as introduced in § IV-3, appears, grows, then starts eroding and finally dies. In order to prevent erosion to start, each individual gives great care avoiding to bring dishonor on his/her family so as not disrupting the family repute. Another honor control mechanism is provided by the Hamingjur, i.e. divinities in charge of keeping the 'luck' of a chosen member of the family where 'luck' means here 'absence of humiliating events within the family'. All this smoothly works as long as the family worships one or several gods who are its glorious roots: these illustrious ancestors cannot accept to acknowledge as a descendant someone who does not live according to his/her ancestors standards. The offspring of the god(dess) or (she)-hero upon which the family has been rooted for several generations constitutes an 'honorable' chain that will maintain high their family standards over the centuries.

Another point that we want to make here is comparing present time definition of mathematical infinity and Norse 'very long durations'. Each reader is welcome to see how his/her own definition of 'eternity' fits or not the mathematical infinite. Without going into details, we may recall this: the mathematical definition of infinity is based on a comparison with the proven infinite set of natural integers. The key idea to build this primary infinite set is to device a function such that, when applied to any integer different from all existing integers, it will create a new integer different from all existing integers (the 'successor' function). This function can be looked at as being the 'generator' of the natural integers infinite family. Mathematicians chose the number zero as being the ancestor of the infinite sequence of natural integers.

Le us now compare this proven mathematical infinity to Norse long duration, and notice deep similarities, even in the way they fail being eternal. As above said, mathematical 0 does not represent at all our 'nothing': it is defined as the original 'father' upon which the existence of each natural number is built.

As much as it may seem ridiculous to identify a god with mathematical zero because of the social prejudice associated in everyday language to someone who is "not much more than a zero," it is striking that Óðinn might have been called "all-father," that is the germ from which all family lines have been built, including all non-kingly ones. As we know, many other figures, such as Þórr, Freyja and various heroes must have been symbols of the august figure of being mother or father of all. These great fecund characters generated various families each element of which has been obtained by a pleasurable successor function, that of sexual reproduction. This feature is similar to the creation of natural numbers in each of the various families, from a unique application of the mathematical successor function. The only important difference between family members and families of numbers is that nothing ensures that a human offspring will be different from all others, though the genetic mechanism makes it highly improbable.

Norse marriage laws, besides, seem to have been imposing extremely strong conditions on the consanguinity of the potential spouses, as if lawyers had been consciously aware of the necessity to ensure that their offspring would be different from all existing ones.

Taking into account this long chain of ancestors, each individual is aware how much honorable is it to inherit of the moral standards of his/her ancestors and is almost forced into an honorable way of life he/she will pass on to his/her own children. All this is in complete accordance with the existence of a Norse religion based on an ancestor cult.

Norse people have certainly not been influenced by the mathematics of natural numbers but we observe here a much deeper potential influence than one issued by some prophet proclaimed religion. Even more, Norse people seem to have realized the transience of all human constructions and felt it necessary to include a huge change, a needed one when humankind would lose the capacity to generate unique individuals, thus the need to create a 'brutally' modified new one. As told by Völuspá, this change is carried on by 'Giants', that is the primitive forces of Nature.

We may now capitalize on our new confidence in Edda poems as reflecting the Norse worldview the poets implicitly have put inside these poems, as we have tried to achieve in chapter III. It is quite noticeable that the suggested influences aim at unveiling the use of a Christian myth, belief or behavior, while our objections to them actually unveil similar behaviors playing a similar role, though now 'typical' of the Norse view of the world. In a sense, all this simply illustrates how much a pagan worldview is repulsive to Christian centered persons. In spite of this repulsion, Norse longhouses and Christian churches have in common to be buildings in which people could meet together, which implies some common taste for these gatherings, without implying the least reciprocal influence.

Conclusion 3

This last chapter is implicitly a literary confirmation of Jung's sentence cited in the Forewords, stating that "magical" means everything where unconscious influences are at work. We have been also reviewing several features of 'typical' pagan Norsemen, some introduced by the mythology, some by Poetic Edda and some by comparing C. Jung sharp analyses of 'eternal' unconscious behaviors and picking out which image they take in the Pagan Norse civilization. Inversely, in § II conclusion, we used Jung's' image of conflicting conscious and unconscious psyches to illustrate how modern advertisement and propaganda might be considered as sendings of the same nature as ancient Norse sköp.

The most unexpected of old Norse features we unveiled is perhaps the one of 'Active introspection' since it is totally absent (as far as we know) of the comments produced by academic commentators though it has been available on this author personal site since more than ten years ago and on Academia.com since 2 or 3 years. The simple approach of considering the possible meaning of some of Hávamál stanzas as compared to other stanzas renders obvious that Hávamál describes complex ways of thinking related to something similar to our introspection though it also deals with a kind of self-friendship similar to the friendship so much described and highly recommended within Hávamál. In some sense, we discovered that ancient Norse thinking took there a way that has been left unexplored (again as far as we know!) by our great philosophers.

In order to properly deal with the 'active introspection' archetype we could not avoid somewhat addressing the 'life and death' archetype because living and dying, and being offered to oneself as claimed by Óðinn in Hávamál s. 138 implies relations with life and death fundamentally differ-ent from our modern ones. We also grieve at having been unable to better deal with the all-encompassing topic of death and life.

In dealing with the Ragnarök archetype we did not try to insist on its various facets since we felt that modern readers are still uneasy with this topic. It is also a modern problem since at least the media seems to be flab-bergasted by their recent discovery of global warming and the most aware political leaders start at best faking to take it into account. Our goal has mainly been to show that its Norse existence is strongly linked to an ances-tors' cult typical of their civilization.

In § IV-4, we compared the five basic features of humankind as described by Völuspá s. 17 and 18 and the ones proposed by C. Jung in his book on the dynamic of psyche. It follows that these ferocious Víkingar have been most identical to anyone of humankind except in two striking exceptions:

– Their belief in their intricate relationship with örlög… a basic topic of this book as explained at length in chapters I and II.

– Their belief in the power of sköp associated to their belief in örlög (and to their ignorance of the world-web!) that prevented them to become too much destructive, as explained in § II-21, sections relative to örlög and sköp.

We finally have been studying a disputed topic, the one of Frigg's responsibility in Baldr's death, where we tried to find a slightly different explanation than Jung's, when Frigg was weakened enough to let leak the information enabling mistletoe to be harmful to her son. Together with Oðinn's active introspection, Frigg's unconscious blunders hints at a pagan Norse civilization the spirituality and psychologic standards to which most commentators seem to have been blind.

We cannot end without citing our analysis of Hávamál s. 27 in which a Galdralag has been astutely imbedded in an apparently irregular Ljóðaháttr, and Sigurðarkviða in skamma s. 142 where a Galdralag has been imbedded in between the two lines of a regular Fornyrðislag. There was something fishy in these stanzas and trying to explained it we did catch very interesting fishes!

As a last fish, here is a kind of 'good sköp', which is nothing but a version of Hávamál s. 141. In both versions the alliterations—as I understood their role—are in bold.

s. 141

Þá nam ek frævask	Then started I to **w**ax
*ok fróðr **v**era*	and full of knowledge **w**as
*ok **v**axa ok **v**el hafask,*	**well** grew and **well** throve,
orð *mér af* **orð**i	a **word** out of my **word**
orðs *leitaði,*	a **word** looked for help
verk *mér af* **verk**i	a **deed** out of my **deed**
verk *leitaði.*	a **deed** looked for help.

Bibliography

The dictionaries used are presented in the introduction.
Old Norse texts were obtained from several sources: Rask's, Jonson's, Dronke's, Lassen's versions and anonymous internet versions.

Beck A. S. (2014): "Opening Doors – Entering Social Understandings of the Viking Age Longhouse" available at https://www.academia.edu/8438640/A._S._Beck_2014_Opening_doors_-_Entering_Social_Understanding_of_the_Viking_Age_Long_House._I_M._S._Kristiansen_and_K._Giles_red._Dwellings_Identities_and_Homes._European_Housing_Culture_from_the_Viking_Age_to_the_Renaissance._H%C3%B8jbjerg_Jysk_Ark%C3%A6ologisk_Selskab._127-138.

"Cold counsel – Women in Old Norse Literature and Mythology," Sarah M. Anderson and Karen Swenson (eds.) Routledge 2002.

Boyer Régis (1992): "L'Edda poétique," Fayard.

Carstens Lydia (2015): "Powerful space. The Iron-Age hall and its development," in Viking Worlds, Things, Spaces, and Movement, pp. 12–27.

Dillmann François-Xavier (2006): "Les magiciens dans l'Islande ancienne," Société des études nordiques.

Dronke Ursula, "The Poetic Edda" Volume I Clarendon Press (1969), II Clarendon Press (1997), III Oxford Univ. Press (2011).

Eriksen Marianne Hem, "Architecture, Society and Ritual in Viking age Scandinavia," 2019.

Evans David (1986): available at http://www.vsnrweb-publications.org.uk/Text%20S.../Havamal.pdf.

Franova Marta & Kodratoff Yves 2017: https://www.academia.edu/35169002/Symbiosis_paper_Intelli_2017.

'Hávamál': http://www.nordic-life.org/nmh/ALLNewHavamalEng.htm OR https://www.academia.edu/40325801/H%C3%A1vam%C3%A1ll_English_translation.

'Hervör's myth': http://www.nordic-life.org/nmh/HervorsMyth.htm OR https://www.academia.edu/40326288/Daring_Herv%C3%B6r_visits_her_fathers_burial_mound.

Hrafnagaldur Óðins: http://www.nordic-life.org/nmh/HRAFENGNEW.htm OR https://www.academia.edu/36097347/HRAFNAGALDUR_%C3%93%C4%90INS_%C3%93%C3%B0inns_Ravens_Galdr_ **and see:** Lassen.

'Hrafnagaldur Óðins', https://www.nordic-life.org/nmh/HRAFENGNEW.htm OR https://www.academia.edu/36097347/HRAFNAGALDUR_%C3%93%C4%90INS_%C3%93%C3%B0inns_Ravens_Galdr_

'Huginn and Muninn': http://www.nordic-life.org/nmh/HuginnMuninnSiteEng.pdf OR https://www.academia.edu/36079086/Huginn_and_Muninn_or_a_few_Archetypes_of_Old_Norse_Collective_Unconscious.

Jackson Elizabeth 1999: "Scáro á scíði örlög seggja: The composition of Völospá 20 and the Implications of the Hauksbók Variant," alvíssmál 9 (1999) pp. 73–88, available at http://userpage.fu-berlin.de/~alvismal/9scaro.pdf.

Jónsson Finnur, "Den Norsk-Islandske Skaldedigtning", Gyldenalske Boghandel, 1908–1912.

Jung C. G. (1966): "Two Essays on Analytical Psychology" p. 153.

Jung C. G. (1967): "Symbols of Transformation," Volume 5 of Bollingen series **XX**.

Jung C. G (1980): "The Archetypes and the Collective Unconscious," (first ed. 1959).

Jung C. G. (1995): "Memories, Dreams, Reflections," Fontana Press (first ed. 1963).

Jung C. G. (2014): "The Structure and Dynamics of the Psyche" Routledge, second edition (first ed. 1960).

Kodratoff Yves & Franova Marta 2019: https://www.academia.edu/38994615/Resonance_Thinking_and_Inductive_Machine_Learning.

'Quiet Draugar': http://www.nordic-life.org/nmh/DraugarQuietOnes. htm OR https://www.academia.edu/40326505/On_the_mythical_ reality_of_quiet_Scandinavian_draugar.

Larrington Carolyne (1993): "A Store of Common Sense," Clarendon Press Oxford.

Larrington Carolyne (2014): "The Poetic Edda, (revised edition)" Oxford University Press.

Lassen Annette "Hrafnagaldur Odins" (2011): available at http://www. vsnrweb-publications.org.uk/Text%20Series/Hrafnagaldur%20 Odins.pdf.

Moen Marianne, PhD thesis 2019: "Challenging_Gender_a_reconsideration_of.pdf" available on Academia.edu.

'Nibelung's three Curses': http://www.nordic-life.org/nmh/Nibelungs ThreeCurses.htm. OR https://www.academia.edu/40326158/ Andvari_Loki_and_F%C3%A1fnir_curse_Nibelungs_Gold.

'NordAp': "The Northern Apocalypse", Terry Gunnell and Annette Lassen (eds) Brepols (2013).

Norddeide Sæbjørg Walaker, "The Viking Age as a Period of Religious Transformation," Brepols, 2011.

Orchard Andy, translation of "The Elder Edda," Penguin, 2011.

Rask Rasmus Kristian, "Edda Sæmundar hinns Fróda", Holmiæ 1818.

Snorri Sturluson, "Edda" (Faulkes' translation) Everyman (1987).

'tale of Völundr': http://www.nordic-life.org/MNG/VolTaleIllustEng.pdf.

"Viking Worlds," Eriksen, Pedersen, Rundberget, Axelsen, Berg (eds), Oxbow Books (2015).

'Völuspá': http://www.nordic-life.org/nmh/VoluPagaEng.htm OR https://www.academia.edu/40325942/VoluPagaEng.

von See Klaus: "Edda, Saga, Skaldendichtung" 1981.

CPSIA information can be obtained
at www.ICGtesting.com
Printed in the USA
LVHW061836130323
741465LV00056B/671

9 781627 342902